ESSENTIAL MANAGERS

MANA[illegible] YOUR [illegible]OSS

CHRISTINA OSBORNE

LONDON, NEW YORK, MUNICH,
MELBOURNE, AND DELHI

DK LONDON

Project Editor Nicky Munro
US Editor Margaret Parrish
DTP Designer Rajen Shah
Production Controller Kevin Ward
Managing Editor Adèle Hayward
Managing Art Editor Karen Self
Category Publisher Stephanie Jackson

DK DELHI

Project Editor Sheema Mookherjee
Editor Rimli Borooah
Project Art Editor Kavita Dutta
DTP Designer Balwant Singh
Managing Editor Ira Pande
Managing Art Editor Aparna Sharma
Editorial Consultant Anita Roy

First American Edition 2003
Published in the United States by
DK Publishing, Inc.
375 Hudson Street
New York, New York 10014

05 06 07 08 10 9 8 7 6 5 4

A Cataloging-in-Publication record for this book is available from the Library of Congress

ISBN 0-7894-9538-4

Color reproduction by Colourscan, Singapore

Printed and bound in China by WKT

See our complete product line at
www.dk.com

CONTENTS

Managing Conflict

Improving Your Prospects

INTRODUCTION

Your relationship with your boss is one of the most important factors in achieving a successful career. Understanding how your boss thinks and works is the key to building a productive partnership. Managing Your Boss *explains how you can get the best out of your boss, whether you are working under pressure or on routine tasks. It shows you how to assess the type of boss you have, suggests how to meet the challenges of working with a difficult boss, and teaches you how to play to your boss's strengths and weaknesses. Practical advice is given to help you define your goals and pursue self-development. A self-assessment questionnaire evaluates how well you manage your boss. Packed with 101 tips, this book will help you turn your boss into your greatest advocate.*

ASSESSING YOUR SITUATION

You can only be effective in your job if you learn to manage your boss. Assess what you want in your career and what you need from your boss so that you can work jointly to reach your goals.

FORMING AN ALLIANCE

You and your boss need each other to succeed, and your relationship is of vital importance. Learn from, and manage this useful ally, so that you can work together effectively as a team, gain job satisfaction, and achieve your career goals.

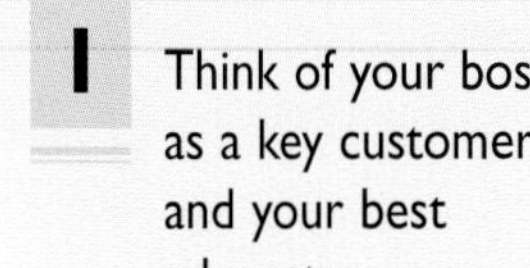

1 Think of your boss as a key customer and your best advocate.

MANAGING YOUR FUTURE

You are responsible for your career development and for being effective in your current job. Your boss and others can help you, but ultimately you manage your own future. Learn to manage your relationship with your boss and remember that she is only human and may need some help. Assess your own and your boss's strengths and weaknesses and jot down areas that need development. Although your boss may not be ideal, make the best of what is likely to be a transitional situation. If you have a good boss, take full advantage of the period during which you are working together.

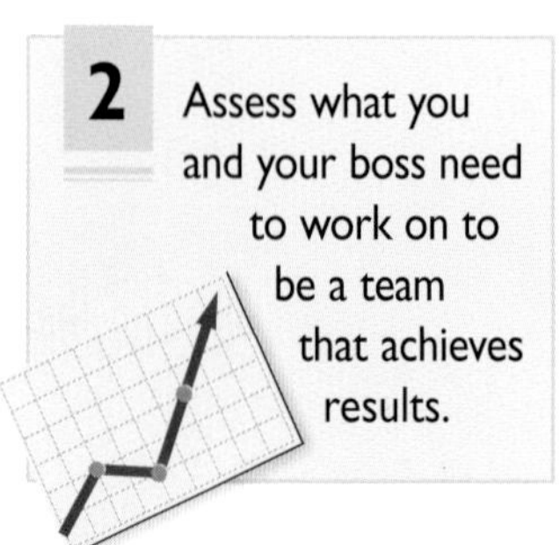

2 Assess what you and your boss need to work on to be a team that achieves results.

ASPIRING FOR THE TOP ▼

In a flat organizational hierarchy that has few management layers you need to stand out as exceptionally competent to get a promotion.
In an organization with just three hierarchical layers, there will be intense competition among peers in the lower layers.

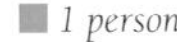

1 person · 15 people · 300 people

LEARNING FROM YOUR BOSS

If you succeed, your boss has a greater chance of success. If your boss is successful, you will be seen as part of a winning team. Bosses like to be known for producing winners. An experienced boss can teach you good judgment in different situations. The contacts that your boss has made can be very useful to you in your career. Be clear to your boss about what help you need to excel at your job, and do not be too proud to take it.

POINTS TO REMEMBER

- Awareness of your own abilities and goals helps you manage your relationship with your boss.
- Although your boss can help you to succeed, you are ultimately responsible for your own future.
- You should learn as much as you can from an efficient boss.

3 Acquire your boss's skills by observation.

▼ GAINING KNOWLEDGE

Your boss probably has wider and more depth of experience than you. Learn from your boss—encourage her to pass on to you job knowledge and understanding of how the organization works.

ASSESSING YOURSELF

When you and your boss share important values and goals, you are more likely to succeed in your job. Understand yourself and what you want out of life and your career, and then ask your boss for help in working toward those goals.

4 Match your goals—professional and personal—to your values.

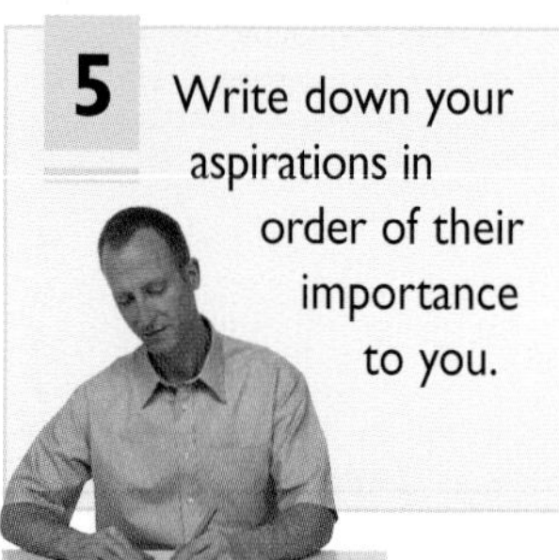

5 Write down your aspirations in order of their importance to you.

DETERMINING VALUES

Be clear about the values that are important to you and decide which career or organization will be compatible with them. Your boss can understand your motivation only if you know what your priorities are. Think about what is important to you and listen to your feelings. Talk to family and friends about what you would like to achieve and where your uncertainties lie. As you explain, listen carefully to your own choice of words. They can reveal what you really feel about your stated goals.

DETERMINING YOUR VALUES AND GOALS

VALUES	GOALS
BUILDING WEALTH	Accumulate assets of $500,000 within 10 years.
CAREER ADVANCEMENT	Gain recognition as an expert in my field within five years.
HEALTHY LIFESTYLE	Have a balanced diet and exercise regularly.
SECURITY	Pay off all my debts within two years.
QUALITY TIME WITH FAMILY	Ensure all weekends off and four weeks vacation per year.
SPIRITUAL RENEWAL	Set aside 15 minutes daily to meditate.

SETTING YOUR GOALS

Being sure about your goals will help you to discuss with your boss, when the time comes, what you want from your career and how he can help you to achieve your goals. Make a comprehensive list of goals in all the areas of your life—for example, in work, learning, or relationships—because each one affects your personal work-life balance and the extent to which you can expect your boss's help.

6 Think of goals associated with your mind, body, heart, and spirit.

▼ **VISUALIZING GOALS**

Close your eyes and think of your goals—a prestigious job, wealth, family. Imagine you have achieved them. Are you happy and are these the right goals? Note what you have learned by looking at your future.

MAKING CHOICES

By visualizing the future, you will identify a number of goals. If you have too many different goals, you will need to prioritize them. Some may be incompatible with others, or with your view of life. Once you are clear about what is important to you, you may set upon a different path in job or change careers altogether.

Goals	A	B	C
Minimum salary $65,000 per annum plus bonus	8	6	3
Career development potential	7	9	4
Interesting and challenging job	5	8	7
Commuting to work less than 30 minutes per day	2	5	9
Opportunity to gain further qualifications	8	8	5
Build on my sector experience	6	8	7
TOTAL	36	44	35

Key to Career Options: A: Global Enterprises Inc.
B: National Organization
C: Local Company

Score out of 10 indicates B is nearest to ideal

◀ **ANALYZING YOUR OPTIONS**

On a sheet of paper, list your goals on the left, and create columns for different career options. Give a score out of 10 against each goal. Add up each column to choose the best career.

Assessing Your Boss Type

Throughout your career you are likely to work for different bosses. Assess which of the following bosses—ideal and less than ideal—most closely match your boss's style, in order to understand effective techniques for managing your type of boss.

7 Change the way you manage your boss according to his or her type.

8 Gain respect from your colleagues by pleasing the perfectionist boss.

The Ideal Boss

Draw up a specification of the ideal boss and review your own situation. If your current boss does not measure up to your ideal, you can identify areas for development. A successful boss has a clear vision of where he and his organization are going, and is interesting and inspiring to work with. He sets high standards for himself as well as for others. His organization skills are excellent, and he delegates effectively by motivating his team to work well. The ideal boss is self-confident and supportive of his team. He is aware of the need to give praise and recognition to others. Before your next career move, assess at the interview how well your potential boss meets these criteria and select a job with the nearest to ideal boss.

▼ **GAINING YOUR COMMITMENT**

A good boss encourages in you a sense of responsibility for ongoing work, and develops your ability to manage yourself and take ownership of projects. This style leads to greater commitment from you than if your boss just tells you what to do.

Your Boss's Style

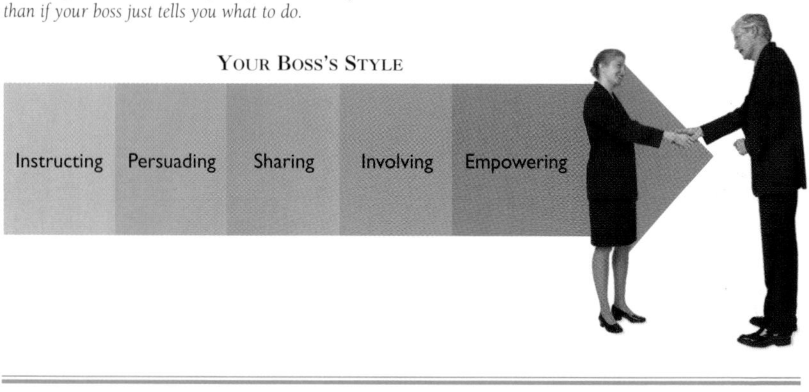

THE PERFECTIONIST BOSS

A perfectionist takes high standards to the extreme and is difficult to please. She is reluctant to delegate in case you fall short of all-around excellence, and is likely to spot anything wrong, from a typing error to noncompliance with procedures. This boss works best in an ordered environment with few interruptions. Recognize her need to feel in control and valued for her expertise by giving frequent progress reports.

9 Advise your boss of any problem as early as possible.

QUESTIONS TO ASK YOURSELF

Q Does my boss communicate effectively with the team as well as outsiders?

Q Does my boss have a good track record at his current and previous jobs?

Q Does my boss make team members feel a sense of responsibility for ongoing projects?

Q Does my boss inspire me to feel a greater sense of commitment toward my work?

THE CHAOTIC BOSS

This boss is often unfocused and moves from one idea to the next instead of following one through. His in-tray is left unattended and his tasks are not delegated. However, he is usually enthusiastic about people and knowledge and can be helpful and informative. Utilize these strengths while you reduce his workload. Leave him with minimal paperwork and meet him briefly every day to plan and decide the crucial tasks to be delegated to you.

▼ UNDERSTANDING GENDER

Although it would be wrong to assess particular managers by generalizing about typical female and male traits, there are broad patterns that are characteristic of each gender.

THE INTERFERING BOSS

A boss who interferes cannot resist checking on the progress of delegated tasks and will hover around your desk. This boss is afraid that if things go wrong, you will not tell him until it is too late. Keeping him regularly updated may not be enough. Difficult as it may seem, ask him to look closely at your work, approach, and progress. He should see that you get on with your work competently and efficiently without his constant input, and will realize that such tight control is unnecessary.

Boss assigns project to team member

Team member keeps boss regularly informed on progress

Boss asks team member for feedback on project frequently, but does not receive regular updates

▲ **HANDLING INTERFERENCE**

With an interfering boss, you will be closely supervised—learn not to be irritated by it. Indulge your boss's need to know every aspect of ongoing projects and eventually he will be convinced that you can be trusted.

10 Win over the trust of the interfering boss.

THE ABSENTEE BOSS

A boss who never seems to be there when you need her moves from one task to another, enjoys trouble-shooting, and is always disappearing to sort out a crisis. She assimilates information quickly and expects others to do the same. This boss expects you to use your initiative and thinks she has given adequate direction. Build relationships with others who work closely with her to obtain information that she has not been around to supply. Ask your boss for her guidance and support to help you carry out delegated tasks. Learn to give short, focused updates, and be persistent in striving for two-way communication.

Boss trusts employee and allows him to work without constant interference

Boss observes that employee is successfully carrying out tasks on his own

The Aggressive Boss

If your boss has outbursts when under stress, learn to handle the aggression. He has plenty of energy and drive that can be channeled constructively. The aggressive boss is used to people agreeing with him, and is intimidating when faced with dissent. When this boss launches into a tirade, stand your ground firmly and suggest a meeting later to explain how you felt about his manner. Emphasize how important it is to you to prevent the recurrence of such an attack as it is demotivating and upsetting, and see if his behavior can change.

Boss loses trust in team member and feels unable to delegate important work

Dos and Don'ts

- ✔ Do check up on the staff turnover of a potential boss.
- ✔ Do praise decisions your boss makes.
- ✔ Do ask for a decision well before it is due if your boss takes a long time to decide.

- ✗ Don't ask a reluctant boss to make too many decisions.
- ✗ Don't suggest a meeting time without looking at your boss's schedule.
- ✗ Don't forget to check how your boss likes to receive information.

The Reluctant Boss

A boss who is reluctant wants to be liked and is slow to make any decision that might cause conflict. You will receive plenty of praise but no negative feedback, however constructive. The most you can expect are general comments about your work. Ask her for feedback and show her that you react well. This boss avoids prioritizing and puts off decisions for fear of adverse results. Take the initiative and make decisions, with the basics agreed upon beforehand. You can gain autonomy and experience working with this type of boss.

11 Agree on the amount of time you need for help.

12 Prompt the reluctant boss to make decisions.

RESPONDING TO YOUR BOSS

The ideal boss is assertive and easy to respond to in the same way. When you are faced with an aggressive or passive boss, assess your habitual response. You may choose to react in the same way or be more constructive and assertive than your boss.

13 Discuss matters with an aggressive boss only after the outburst is over.

FACING AGGRESSION

A directly aggressive boss lets her anger out, perhaps by shouting at you if you make a mistake. Assess whether you can cope with this by mentally withdrawing each time it happens. Deal with the situation by maintaining eye contact, remaining calm, and waiting for her anger to subside. She may even apologize soon afterward. If this does not work, point out that shouting is not helping either of you, and suggest that you talk through the problem in private when she is calmer.

◀ **STOPPING THE TIRADE**
If all else fails, you may have to resort to surprise tactics to halt your boss's tirade. Say her name loudly to interrupt her and give yourself a chance to speak.

RECOGNIZING INDIRECT AGGRESSION

An indirectly aggressive boss lets her anger out in subtle ways—for example, by making sarcastic comments, or being more resistant to your ideas than usual. She is taking the indirect route instead of confronting you. In the worst possible instance, you may hear rumors or overhear your boss complaining about your work. Assess your response quickly. Tackle the situation before it escalates further, especially if you find yourself being left out of important decisions. At a one-on-one meeting with your boss, discuss your feelings, ask questions to help you understand the problem, and propose a way forward.

HELPING A PASSIVE BOSS

A passive boss avoids confrontation and fails to tackle awkward situations. He appears calm but can be just as difficult to deal with as an aggressive boss. This kind of boss has an excessive desire to please his superiors and will procrastinate for fear of failure. Your response to him should be assertive and cooperative. Encourage him to meet with you to review progress—he will agree to this since he wants to appear helpful. Help him to voice his concerns by asking open questions assertively.

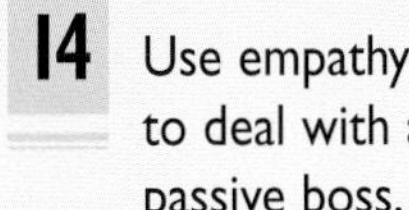

14 Use empathy to deal with a passive boss.

HANDLING PASSIVITY

With a passive boss, you may need to use your own initiative to solve problems. Do this as tactfully as possible so that your boss does not mind you speaking up.

Boss is silent at a crucial stage of talks with client

Client is concerned at lack of progress

Team member makes suggestion and moves the discussion forward

THINGS TO DO

1. Think about how you can change your habitual response to your boss.
2. Ask for time to think about what your boss has said if you feel that you need to.
3. Anticipate a positive response from your boss and you may get it.

BEING MUTUALLY ASSERTIVE

The assertive boss has a realistic view of himself and others. He is easy to respond to assertively as he makes you feel you have a valued contribution to make. Aggressive or passive bosses ignore the rights of others to be listened to and to express their own opinions. An assertive boss listens to you with an open mind. If he disagrees, he does so in a constructive way, without attacking you verbally or manipulating your reply. You can behave assertively and say what you feel, even if you disagree, as you work together toward a solution.

MAKING THE MOST OF DELEGATION

A crucial management skill affecting your situation at work, delegation is the key to your boss's effective management of you. If your boss is a good manager, she will also be a good delegator, and together you will be a productive and efficient team.

15 Accept routine tasks, but minimize the time you spend on them.

16 Be enthusiastic about taking on responsibilities.

17 Negotiate realistic deadlines for new tasks.

TAKING THE CUE FROM YOUR BOSS

Your boss should have the professional skills needed at her level, and be committed to the development of her team members. Observing how your boss manages you and others will give you insights into the way you like or do not like to be managed. Managers ensure tasks are done through others, and it is important to assess your boss's delegating skills. Consider whether you have the opportunity to learn from her, and to use your newly acquired knowledge and skills.

CASE STUDY

Angela Everett worked in a profitable niche business built on the charismatic founder's personal qualities. She had been brought in to structure the company for further growth. The new management team was finding it difficult to work effectively because Angela's boss insisted on making key customer decisions. Angela organized an externally facilitated session with the boss and the management team. Together they reviewed goals and responsibilities, and debated the risks of devolving some of the key responsibilities the boss had retained. This honest review enabled the company to utilize the boss's undoubted personal charisma on PR and other high-profile activities. The management team made sure this was backed by effective customer service and operations. Turnover increased and within three years the company expanded threefold.

REVIEWING ROLES ▶
The founder of a successful company was now a constraint on its growth. Open discussion with his team led him to trust his managers to work within clear lines of responsibility.

ASSESSING YOUR BOSS AS A DELEGATOR

Ask yourself these questions about your boss. If you answer mostly "no", you may need to manage your boss so that, over time, she understands that virtually everything—except strategy or elements of her role that concern leading her team—could be delegated to you.

"Does my boss realize that being in control does not mean she has to make all the decisions?"

"Does she take the time to help me develop the skills I need to perform a delegated task well?"

"Is my boss secure enough not to be worried about her own position if I perform delegated tasks well?"

"Does my boss delegate the whole job to me, giving me full authority to make decisions?"

ACCEPTING DELEGATION

You can influence how much work your boss delegates to you. Even if you suspect she only passes on the tasks that she least likes, you can manage her to become a better delegator. Encourage an unwilling delegator at first by accepting the most routine tasks. Make sure that you meet the deadlines and standards set by your boss. Give her feedback on your progress and ask if there is more work that you can take off her hands. As you prove that you are competent, your boss will entrust you with more and more responsible tasks.

DELEGATING TOO MUCH
Some bosses delegate all aspects of their job. While this may be a good chance to prove yourself, assess whether you have the required skills and time to perform these tasks.

18 Ensure that you are given authority along with additional responsibility.

REVIEWING YOUR CURRENT RELATIONSHIP

People who work together can fall into a fixed routine. As organizational goals move on and you develop, assess if your and your boss's behavior patterns are still effective. If not, help your boss to accept that the current relationship needs to change.

19 Change yourself rather than expect your boss to change.

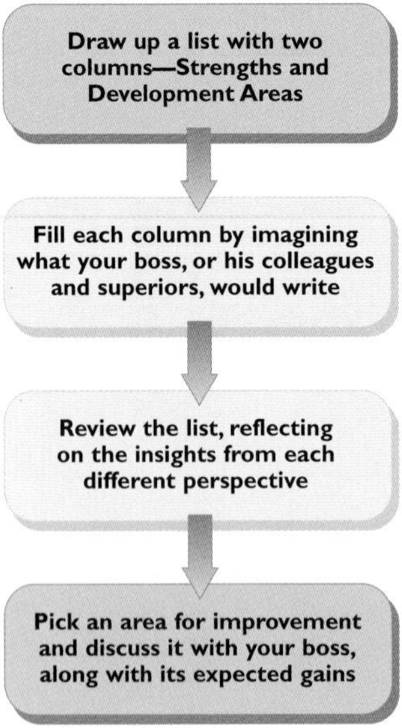

Draw up a list with two columns—Strengths and Development Areas

↓

Fill each column by imagining what your boss, or his colleagues and superiors, would write

↓

Review the list, reflecting on the insights from each different perspective

↓

Pick an area for improvement and discuss it with your boss, along with its expected gains

▲ EXPLORING DIFFERENT PERSPECTIVES

Look at how you and your boss work together from viewpoints other than your own. Collate the different perspectives and work systematically through each development area with your boss.

ASSESSING WHAT NEEDS TO CHANGE

Focus on the objectives that you and your boss are responsible for achieving in the organization. Review how you tackle these responsibilities together and identify when your relationship works well or not so well. Be specific about what you want to change. Ask questions about what helps and what hinders you and your boss at work and prepare practical suggestions, with benefits for both of you, to raise in discussion.

DOS AND DON'TS

- ✔ Do expect to continuously improve in your job.
- ✔ Do seek to understand your boss's perspective.
- ✔ Do look for a win-win solution for both you and your boss.
- ✔ Do review your existing relationship with your boss, especially if you feel nothing has changed for some time.

- ✘ Don't act without anticipating what your boss might think.
- ✘ Don't take your boss for granted.
- ✘ Don't resist change without considering the consequences fully.
- ✘ Don't forget to review with your boss what the two of you have learned through working together.

MOVING TOWARDS A WIN-WIN SOLUTION

After suggesting a change to your boss, listen to his response. If he does not agree with you, ask questions that entail more than just a yes or no answer, to understand his point of view. Discuss the benefits of your suggestion and be open to alternative proposals. Through a two-way discussion with both of you listening to each other, you can find a win-win solution. If your boss still does not see the need to change, it might be time to start looking for a new job.

20 Identify recurring situations that you can improve.

21 End all discussions with your boss on a positive note.

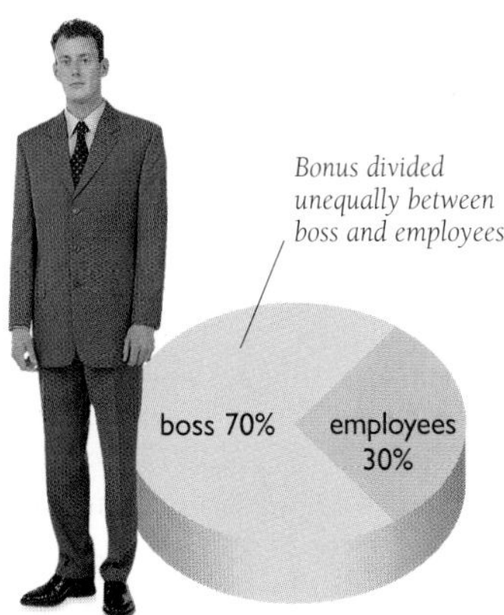

▲ **WINNING AS A TEAM**
An improvement in your working relationship with your boss will make you more effective as a team. Looking for a win-win solution will provide more gains than you could achieve on your own.

22 Give a new boss a fair chance to prove himself.

EXPECTING CHANGE

Some time in the future you or your boss will move on. Be prepared for a new relationship and assess your new boss objectively. If you had a good relationship with your previous boss or worked with him for a long time, it may be difficult to avoid comparing a new boss with the old one. To build a good rapport with your new boss, you will need to appreciate fresh ideas and avoid constantly referring to the past. Both of you will have to invest time to achieve an effective partnership.

Working with Your Boss

Managing your boss begins with managing yourself, performing well, and using initiative. Understand what is important to your boss so that you can help him work well and receive help in return.

Anticipating Needs

Show initiative, and save your boss time, by understanding how he works and anticipating his needs. When you brief your boss on a problem, present your solution at the same time. If your boss is part of the problem, try to give feedback constructively.

23 Think about what your boss needs to know and give frequent updates.

▲ **SETTING UP MEETINGS**
If your boss receives information best by listening, ensure that you have face-to-face meetings supplemented by phone calls.

Knowing Your Boss

It is crucial to know your boss's style of working and be clear how you will communicate with each other. Think about how he prefers to receive information and how frequently. Your boss may be happy with a series of quick meetings to address problems as the need arises. Or he may manage better with structured meetings, asking for an agenda in advance. Find out if your boss takes in facts best by listening, or prefers reading. Ask if he would like to hear a verbal presentation, followed by your report, or if he would prefer to read it first and then ask questions.

KEEPING YOUR BOSS INFORMED

By understanding what information your boss wants and how often he likes feedback, you can keep him up-to-date on important issues and be left alone to do your work. Ask him if he prefers you to give a summary of every aspect of a project, or to report only unexpected results. You may need to go for quick, frequent updates or periodic reviews according to the nature of the project. Your boss's need for information can change, so check whether his needs are being met.

24 Time your reports according to the project stage.

25 Submit reports if your boss prefers written records.

ASSESSING HOW TO COMMUNICATE WITH YOUR BOSS

MEDIUM	PURPOSE	WHEN USEFUL
E-MAIL 	To record communication, and for non-urgent questions.	Your boss is happy to use e-mail and has time to deal with it. Use it when you need a record of your question or want your boss to note an achievement.
 PHONE	To address issues promptly that can be dealt with verbally.	Your boss does not mind interruptions and copes well with quick verbal exchanges. Limit the interruptions by only phoning on important issues.
BRIEF AD-HOC MEETING 	To discuss issues that have just arisen and need urgent attention.	Your boss is happy with quick face-to-face interruptions. Use it when your boss needs some important information or to resolve an urgent issue.
 MEMO	To explain why a document is being sent, or to act as a reminder.	Your boss corresponds by memo and prefers to sort an in-tray of papers rather than deal with e-mail. Use a memo if you need to make a point for the record.
FORMAL MEETING 	To discuss issues face to face, with a preplanned agenda.	Your boss responds well to planned one-on-one meetings. Use these regularly to keep your boss updated on progress and for coaching and two-way feedback.

ANALYZING PROBLEMS

Problems, such as failing to meet deadlines or making ill-advised decisions, reflect poorly on your own and your boss's reputation. Understanding the causes of problems is the first step toward solving them. Collect all the facts about difficulties that recur in the work you and your boss do, or in your relationship, and review them to identify the cause. List all the possible solutions you can think of to tackle the problem. Assess the benefits of each solution from the point of view of your boss and that of the organization. The one with the most benefits is likely to be the best solution for you to present to your boss.

26 Ask yourself what you would change if you could wave a magic wand.

27 Summarize your solution on one sheet of paper for your boss.

CREATING A WINNING PROPOSAL

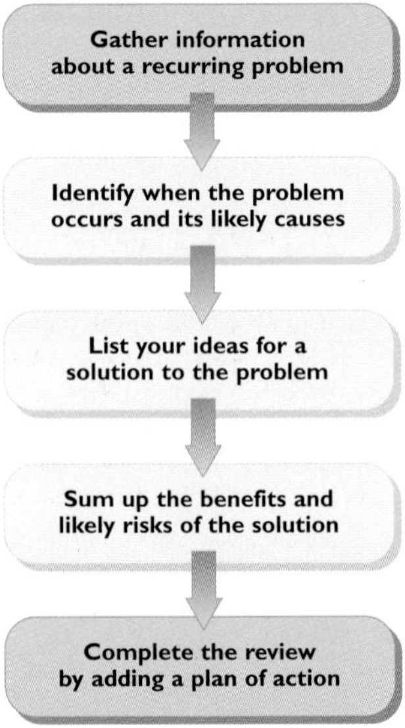

Gather information about a recurring problem

↓

Identify when the problem occurs and its likely causes

↓

List your ideas for a solution to the problem

↓

Sum up the benefits and likely risks of the solution

↓

Complete the review by adding a plan of action

QUESTIONS TO ASK YOURSELF

Q Do I make an effort to find out the causes of problems?

Q Have I gathered information about a recurring problem?

Q Have I identified when the problem occurs?

Q Have I thought about all possible solutions?

Q Am I well prepared to answer any question my boss has?

Q Am I aware of the risks and benefits of my solution?

PRESENTING SOLUTIONS

Prepare a summary of your analysis of the problem, its impact, and likely causes to present to your boss. This will help a methodical boss to check the detail and the logic, especially if he likes to view matters one step at a time. The same summary works equally well for a boss who finds detail tedious, as it gives him an instant overview. Discuss with your boss what needs to be done by whom and by when, and jointly put together an action plan, including review dates, in order to present a complete solution.

RAISING ISSUES

If your boss's weaknesses and your inability to compensate for them are endangering your success as a team, you need to consider whether it is worth addressing the issue with your boss. A frank discussion may benefit you both and help to resolve problems before they become too difficult to handle. However, if you feel that he may react adversely and your job might be at stake, try to ignore the issues that you can live with and raise only those that are vital.

28 Uncover hidden conflicts with your boss before they get out of hand.

29 Raise issues only when your boss can give you full attention.

GIVING FEEDBACK

The willingness of you and your boss to give each other constructive feedback is a measure of the effectiveness of your relationship. Your feedback can be motivational, in the form of praise, or developmental, which focuses on what you see as your boss's shortcomings. This is the hardest feedback to give, so think about what to say and how to phrase it constructively. Write down examples of his behavior and the impact it has on you. Anticipate his reaction and decide whether the benefits of giving feedback outweigh the risks.

▼ **CRITICIZING CONSTRUCTIVELY**

Developmental feedback should be in the form of constructive suggestions rather than hard-hitting criticism.

Employee suggests ways of improving the working partnership

Boss listens carefully to his well-considered points

POINTS TO REMEMBER

- You should gather facts and analyze the causes of a problem you are trying to resolve, before moving on to the solutions.
- Your solutions are more likely to be accepted if you present the benefits to all those affected.
- To be successful, feedback should always be constructive.
- Praise for your team members and boss should be genuine and motivational.

PRESENTING YOURSELF POSITIVELY

Presenting yourself and your work well will create a favorable impression with your boss. Always be positive in all your dealings with your boss—this in turn will help your boss to be upbeat and in the right frame of mind for success.

30 Keep yourself fit to retain energy for work and achieve high productivity.

31 Adopt a good posture and hold your head high.

CREATING A GOOD IMPRESSION

Be aware of the image you project, both by your manner, and the clothes you wear. Positive body language will reassure your boss that you can do the job. Emulate the dress code of people at a level above you. In this way, you project to your boss, and others, the idea that you could fulfill a more senior position and that you have the authority and ambition to succeed. Present your written communications professionally to engender the same confidence in the work that you produce.

LOOKING GOOD ▼

Always appear well-prepared, maintain eye contact, and communicate key points clearly. This will make your boss more receptive to the purpose of your presentation.

Employee presents ideas in a self-assured and professional manner

Boss is impressed with presentation and receptive to new ideas

DOING MORE THAN EXPECTED

Always underpromise and overdeliver rather than the other way round if you want to delight your boss. Doing more than is expected of you will get you noticed and persuade your boss that you are worth investing in for the future. It is reassuring for her to know that you complete work before the deadline and arrive on time for meetings. Be the first to come up with innovative solutions and be a cooperative team member. Keep asking yourself: What else would help my boss?

32 Always think about the consequences of your actions for others.

▼ **INFLUENCING OTHERS**

Through a positive approach, you convey that you are part of a successful team, in turn affecting the attitude of others.

MANAGING MOODS

Your physical expressions can affect your psychological state. Simply smiling will make you feel better. Manage your mood by reflecting on past successes. Help others, including your boss, to value their achievements and feel good about themselves.

FEELING POSITIVE

Your boss will want to be around people who give energy rather than drain it. By always being constructive in your approach, you can renew your boss's energy when work is particularly challenging. Both your roles as leaders, at different levels, involve being inspirational to others. You can maintain morale and motivate the team to achieve objectives by being positive. When stating an objective, let your boss and peers know what you can do rather than what you cannot.

DEFINING BOUNDARIES

You and your boss share the responsibility of developing a successful working relationship. Building good rapport, and defining and understanding the boundaries of each other's roles are the first steps toward an effective partnership.

33 Agree on the boundaries with your boss early in the relationship.

34 Align your goals with those that are most important to your boss.

▼ **CLARIFYING WORK CRITERIA**

Seek your boss's help when setting your objectives and ask him to outline the criteria on which the standard of your work will be judged.

OUTLINING RESPONSIBILITIES

There are many ways in which you can define responsibilities—from employment contracts to outcomes for which you are rewarded. While you should appear flexible to your boss, you also need to understand your job, your responsibilities, and your level of authority. You should know what is expected of you in your role and the criteria that will define your success. In turn, you should also understand your boss's responsibilities and the success criteria for his role.

Boss helps define the responsibilities of employee's job

Employee assesses competencies to be achieved based on the job description

BUILDING RAPPORT

You need to create opportunities to encourage an open relationship with your boss that allows both of you to express your feelings. Meet every two weeks to review progress together so that you can both mention any concerns as part of your usual conversation, rather than having to call a special meeting. Listen encouragingly and empathize with your boss, observing how he might be feeling and noticing any recent change in his manner. When rapport is built, it will be easy to share your observations or to ask for your boss's help.

35 Maintain eye contact with your boss and ask open questions.

◀ **SETTING THE AGENDA**
Reduce any uncertainties at the beginning of a meeting by presenting your items for the agenda and checking what your boss would like to discuss. Agree on the three most important items.

STANDING AGENDA

1. Agree on an Agenda (Listen to each other's suggested agenda items and agree on the three priorities to discuss)
2. Discuss Objective 1
3. Discuss Objective 2
4. Discuss Objective 3
5. Summarize
6. Agree on Action Plan

Stick to three objectives per meeting—you can always meet more often

Summarize actions agreed to, so that you both leave with the same understanding of what is to be done

36 Be clear about what your organization expects of you and your boss.

WORKING IN PARTNERSHIP

A good working relationship combines your resources with those of your boss, so that you achieve together more than either of you could have done alone. Your relationship should accommodate individual creativity and initiative. Find out early on how much of your job you will be expected to manage on your own and how much will be assigned to you by your boss. Your boss may have a different view of the level of autonomy you can exercise on a project over and above the day-to-day administrative tasks associated with your job.

BUILDING TRUST

Trust is built by doing what you say and showing that you can be relied on to deliver set outcomes. This process will go through a trial period during which your boss trusts you until proved wrong, or does not trust you until you have proved yourself.

37 Work on reducing barriers to your boss's trust in your abilities.

38 Ask your boss how you are doing and act on her comments.

PROVING YOURSELF

A trusting boss will expect you to deliver what you promised and will only impose restrictions if you let her down. She might be happy if you explain your approach briefly before you go ahead and give progress reports afterward. A distrusting boss will give you small tests and only let you work unsupervised once you have proven yourself. Plan patiently how you will gain the trust of this kind of boss. Look out for clues that reveal her doubts and work toward resolving them. As trust is built, the brief will be less detailed and the progress reporting less frequent.

Agree on subgoals that achieve overall goals

Document gives overview of progress

PROGRESS REVIEW CHART

Primary Goal	Reviews
Achieve the Zed project to budget and time.	At least monthly or at each project milestone.
Secondary Goals 1. Relocate the filing and library areas without disruption to sales or customer service standards.	**09/22/03** Relocation completed by due date. No complaints about any disruption or lost files.
2. Upgrade the central library access area and implement new filing system.	**10/15/03** Upgrade on target for due date. Chasing for delivery of new filing system—ETA one week late.
3. Organize files to be retrieved from relocated area and arranged in new filing system.	**10/22/03** Next review.

Review chart with your boss at key points

Note what went well or not so well

Set date for next review with your boss

◀ **REVIEWING PROGRESS**
Use a Progress Review Chart to give you and your boss an overview of what has been achieved and to identify any problems at an early stage.

39 Update your boss on your latest achievements and learning.

TAKING THE INITIATIVE

It is a challenge to take the initiative yourself, while also acknowledging your boss. Do what you were hired to do and show a responsible approach. This means checking, finishing, and following-up your own work. Taking the initiative involves all this and more—it means looking around for what else you can do rather than waiting to be told.

40 Offer to take on extra work to help your overloaded boss.

DOS AND DON'TS

- ✔ Do show your boss that you deliver what you promise.
- ✔ Do act quickly if your boss feels you have let her down in some way.
- ✔ Do explain why a job went wrong and ask for help next time.
- ✗ Don't make excuses that aren't real.
- ✗ Don't go your own way without ensuring you have your boss's full support.
- ✗ Don't assume your boss won't notice if something goes wrong.

RETAINING YOUR BOSS'S TRUST

It is important to invest time in maintaining trust between you and your boss. Assess the risks of your boss delegating work to you, and reassure her by explaining how you could control possible risks. If you disagree with your boss, do so in private, unless she asks for your opinion in front of others. If you unintentionally embarrass your boss publicly, apologize immediately. If you sense a misunderstanding, clarify it at a separate meeting. In this way you will minimize the risk of losing your boss's trust when taking the initiative.

◀ **REBUILDING TRUST**

Trust, once broken, must be rebuilt—however difficult it seems. If you fail to meet your boss's expectations in some way, and feel she has suddenly distanced herself, make sure you have a talk with her and clear up any misunderstanding.

COMPLEMENTING YOUR BOSS'S STYLE

You need to make up for your boss's weaknesses and encourage her to delegate to your strengths, so that you become a complementary team. Focus on your boss's priorities, learn to think like her, and impress her with your forward thinking.

41 Understand your organization's goals and objectives to help your boss.

42 Observe how your boss prioritizes tasks.

43 Read up on major customers and competitors.

UNDERSTANDING YOUR BOSS'S PRIORITIES

Your boss has to achieve organizational objectives. Make sure you know what these are. Ask your boss what her priorities are in achieving these objectives and focus your time on these. If your boss focuses on what she enjoys, rather than what is important to the organization, you need to refocus her attention to ensure that you both spend enough time on the right priorities. Find out the challenges your organization faces and keep abreast of the external competition.

THINKING LIKE THE BOSS

If your boss is short of time and seems to rely on telepathy to communicate, it is important for you to learn to think like her. By understanding her goals and values you can match her thoughts even if you lack her experience or knowledge. Assess whether your boss is a right-brained creative person or a left-brained logical one. By observing how she habitually thinks, you can anticipate her decisions in most situations. If your boss is known for her good judgment, getting to know her decision-making techniques will be invaluable.

QUESTIONS TO ASK YOURSELF

Q When I present a new idea, what does my boss look at first—overview or detail?

Q Does my boss make decisions quickly or put them off?

Q Does my boss resist change or welcome new ideas?

Q Does my boss plan ahead with contingency time, or is she taken by surprise by the unexpected?

KNOWING HOW YOUR BOSS'S MIND WORKS

LEFT BRAIN ANALYZES FACTS	RIGHT BRAIN CREATES IDEAS
• Is logical	• Is intuitive
• Thinks in linear steps	• Thinks laterally
• Is analytical	• Views the whole picture
• Needs facts and details	• Admits to feeling emotion
• Observes objectively	• Allows subjective opinions

SUPPORTING YOUR BOSS

Encourage your boss to acknowledge that you both have strengths and weaknesses, and map out where you can complement each other. Learn how much time your boss needs to make a decision and give timely information. Persuade a resistant boss to make necessary changes, and complete unfinished tasks for an unfocused, chaotic boss. Reassure a boss who is nervous about making decisions by recalling previous successful decisions she made. If she stays in her office, encourage her to interact with others and get feedback.

44 Discuss one issue at a time with a single-minded boss.

▼ **COMBINING STRENGTHS**
If your thinking style is the opposite to that of your boss, maximize your differing strengths and work as a complementary team. The two of you will have a rounded view of any situation and the potential for good combined judgment.

MANAGING YOUR WORKLOAD

Your boss will be impressed if you manage your workload efficiently and accomplish important tasks on time. Successful people focus on the right priorities, make optimum use of their time, and do not take on more work than they can handle.

45 Increase the time you allow for tasks if you tend to underestimate.

PRIORITIZING YOUR WORK

Focus on what is important and plan your time realistically, including contingency time for coping with the unexpected. Prioritize your workload—give your most important tasks high priority and delegate as much of your work as you can to leave enough time to meet key deadlines. Bring another priority forward if you complete a task before the deadline.

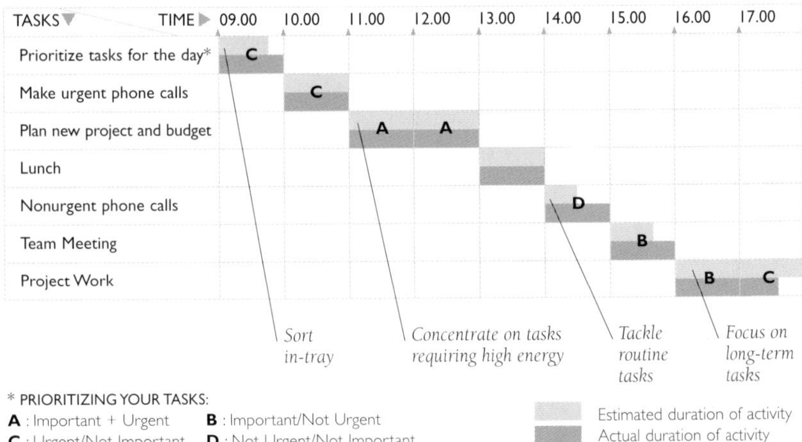

▼ ESTIMATING TIME

Learn to plan your work day efficiently by choosing the best time for different activities. Prioritize the tasks that you have to complete and place them in suitable time slots. Estimate how long each task will take and check the accuracy of your forecast once the jobs are done.

REDUCING INTERRUPTIONS

Frequent interruptions prevent you from focusing on important objectives. Analyze your time to check which activities waste time and who disturbs you most, and plan your day to reduce these distractions. You may keep your office door shut at times during the day. If you work in an open-plan office, establish a mutual signal with your colleagues for times when you do not wish to be disturbed. Keep meetings with your boss and colleagues as short as possible, setting a time limit at the beginning to keep the meeting focused. Think about your boss's time management in the same way, and make sure you are not one of his unnecessary "interruptions."

MEETING BRIEFLY
It is often a good idea to conduct a brief meeting standing up, as this discourages aimless chatting and makes it easier to leave when you have finished.

46 Have your phone calls diverted when you need to concentrate.

47 Explain that you find it difficult, but still say "No" if you need to.

LEARNING TO SAY "NO"

If you have to turn down your boss's request, do so assertively and sensitively. Acknowledge the request and give your reason for being unable to comply. This will usually be because you have a number of other more important priorities that will slip if you take on this extra task. You could outline to your boss all the other tasks you have, so that he can understand your options, and ask what he would do. The best thing is to say "no" as if you mean it—if you try to soften your refusal with excessive apologies or excuses, you will confuse the message. If you are unsure whether you would be able to complete the task, take time to think things through before responding.

Showing Loyalty

Showing loyalty means supporting and promoting your boss and trying to understand and meet his expectations. Your boss should expect you to be loyal until the moment he takes your loyalty for granted and puts you in an uncomfortable situation.

48 Build two-way relationships with people who are important to you.

49 Check out an organization's values and culture before you join.

50 Speak well of your boss as it reflects well on you.

Understanding Reciprocity

The relationship between you and your boss is based on fair concessions on each side. Your boss represents the organization that pays you, directs your work to meet objectives, gives you tools to work with, and provides you with job security. You can also expect to be praised for good work, and be given feedback and training. In return, your boss can expect to receive your commitment to producing work at the standard required and your loyalty to the organization. In addition, your boss can expect you to be reliable and to acknowledge his support and guidance.

Being Loyal

Loyalty entails making your boss look good in public. By working to increase your boss's credibility, you enhance your own position as well as show loyalty. As long as you share the values of your boss and the organization, loyalty is easy. However, if your boss appears to be doing something that makes you uncomfortable, you should ask him for an explanation. You can then assess whether the difficulty arose because you did not understand the situation fully or if your loyalty is being pushed too far.

▲ **BEING OPEN**

If your boss's working style seems to go against your principles, voice your discomfort. Your boss's response will help you assess your allegiance to him.

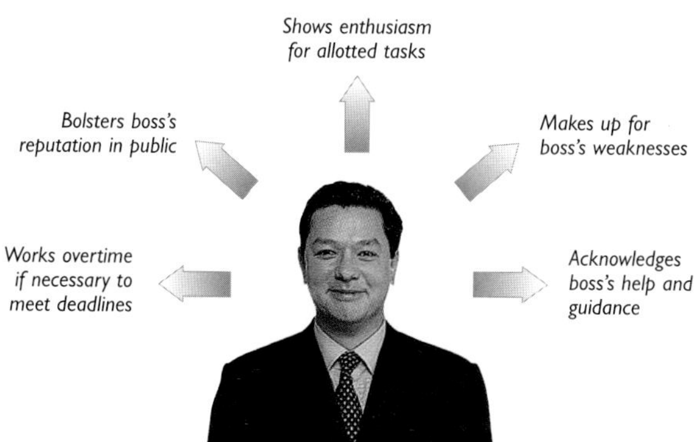

▲ **RECOGNIZING LOYALTY**
A loyal employee is committed to his boss and organization. He will stand by his boss until he feels his loyalty is being pushed too far or that the organization will suffer.

WITHDRAWING LOYALTY

Your loyalty will be tested if your boss is doing something wrong. If he behaves in a way that you disagree with, or that the organization would disapprove of, express your misgivings and give him a chance to change. If the problem continues, you could discuss it with the human resources department. Let your conscience decide how much you can tolerate, but be aware that whistleblowers often pay a personal cost. However, if what your boss is doing is illegal, you may be seen to collude with him if you continue to support him.

51 Be guided by what an objective third party may think.

CASE STUDY

James Kenton was happy in his job and had a good relationship with his boss. However, he was approached by a recruitment agency for a more senior position in an unknown competing company. James was tempted to find out what they would offer but felt loyalty toward his boss and decided to tell her that he had received this offer. His boss's reaction was typically supportive. She told James that she would not like to lose him but did not mind him exploring the new post. James went to the interview and became wary when the headhunter started asking questions about his colleagues. He declined to proceed any further. A few months later his company was taken over by the same competitor and James and his boss were promoted into the new organization. They had checked out his loyalty and discretion beforehand.

GAINING FROM LOYALTY ▶
An employee remains loyal to his present organization during an interview for a new job. He is rewarded unexpectedly for his discretion.

SOCIALIZING WITH YOUR BOSS

The difference in status between you and your boss can make socializing difficult to handle. If it is part of your job to socialize with your boss, understand the boundaries of your friendship—or colleagues may resent your relationship.

52 Talk about neutral subjects such as hobbies and vacations.

53 Learn the art of networking from a successful boss.

▼ **REMAINING ALERT**
When socializing with your boss, avoid too much alcohol and stay alert. People may remember what you have said and read more into your words than you meant.

MAKING SMALL TALK

There is an art to making small talk that does not offend anyone and keeps conversation going. In a social situation, chat about topical issues, but avoid controversial subjects. Concentrate on networking, introducing people, and putting everyone at ease, especially if your boss has invited guests. Change the subject if you are asked personal questions, or for sensitive information about your organization.

▲ **SHARING A SPORT**
Enjoying organized out-of-office sporting activities with your boss and colleagues may help to build on the rapport that you share at work.

KEEPING WITHIN BOUNDARIES

The relationship between you and your boss is a business one, and being overfriendly can blur professional and social boundaries. If your boss is also your friend, it may be more difficult to refuse favors, such as being asked to work late frequently. Although you and your boss may think you can balance your professional and social relationships, others in the organization may think otherwise. Colleagues might suspect favoritism and your boss may feel compelled to overcompensate by being harder on you than others. You need to be aware of all these risks.

MAINTAINING THE BALANCE

You may manage to keep a friendship, as well as working relationship with your boss and your colleagues in balance for many years. However, the situation can alter when new people join the organization or if events change in your or your boss's personal life. View the relationship as objectively as possible. Discuss any potential problems with your boss and, if necessary, ask for his help in planning a career move.

DOS AND DON'TS

- ✔ Do remain professional, however friendly you are with your boss.
- ✔ Do support your boss at social gatherings.
- ✔ Do keep in mind organizational policy on friendships at work.
- ✗ Don't forget others' views on your closeness with your boss.
- ✗ Don't make colleagues feel left out.
- ✗ Don't discuss personal details about your boss if the friendship ends.

CULTURAL DIFFERENCES

In countries such as Sweden, employees and their bosses often socialize within the workplace. Eating together is seen as a natural way to build working relationships. Conversely, in countries with a more formal working culture, such interaction does not take place and bosses tend to eat separately from staff.

54 Recognize that relationships may change.

Managing Conflict

If you ignore conflict, the situation will only get worse. Take action at the first sign of friction, and learn to deal with both negative and positive feedback, and harassment or bullying.

Resolving Conflict

Difficult situations must be handled carefully. Be alert for signs of conflict and analyze what is happening. Keep your own responses in check, while you explore with your boss ways in which you can work together to resolve the problem.

55 Understand how your boss usually reacts and spot changes early.

56 Ensure that your boss regards you as supportive.

57 Note your boss's body language—it is a good indicator of likely conflict.

Observing the Signs

A potential cause of conflict is your manager's insecurity about her position as you gain recognition within the organization. You may be tempted to compete with her but you will achieve more by working with her active cooperation. Look out for signs of any problems, verbal and nonverbal. If your boss seems unusually irritated with you or finds fault with your decision on a minor issue, this could be an early warning signal of impending conflict. Other signs to alert you of an imminent outburst from your boss are foot- or pencil-tapping, and pacing up and down.

THINGS TO DO

1. Act soon if changes in your boss's behavior worry you.
2. Use "I" statements to tell your boss how you feel.
3. Give your boss a way to save face if she is wrong.

DISCUSSING THE PROBLEM

To discover the root of any conflict, arrange a meeting when you feel your boss is in a calm frame of mind. You may find it daunting to be open with her, but honesty about how you feel is a good starting point. Your boss will probably wish to appear reasonable by hearing you out patiently. Encourage her to bring to the surface any hidden conflict by asking for her feedback.

▼ **RESPONDING WELL**

In some conflict situations, you may need to stand up to your boss. Be assertive rather than aggressive.

Team member gives boss a written report the next day and she is pleased with the way he has dealt with the problem

Boss is unusually critical of team member's handling of a project at a meeting

Team member responds assertively, giving a quick summary of the progress so far

Team member reacts angrily

Boss is displeased at what she sees as disloyal behavior and their working relationship is damaged

TACKLING THE SITUATION

Review the way in which you and your boss deal with problems. Do you usually shy away from conflict, or do you enjoy it? Avoiding conflict will not resolve problems and hinders your joint effectiveness. A continuous spiral of attack and defense is not helpful either. Define the problem and explain the impact it has on you, without resorting to blame. Listen carefully to your boss's opinions and feelings before summarizing points of agreement and suggestions for action.

RECEIVING FEEDBACK

Feedback on your work can come from your boss, colleagues, and customers, through a formal appraisal, or informally. You need to be able to accept and make use of feedback—whether it is praise or criticism—without it leading to conflict.

58 Make use of feedback to develop and change your role.

59 Be aware of all the responsibilities of your current position.

60 Identify all possible routes for future career growth.

PREPARING FOR APPRAISALS

If you dread appraisals because you have disagreed in the past with the comments made by your boss, change your approach before the next one. View appraisals as an opportunity to help your boss to recognize your successes or to recommend you for promotion. Between appraisals, make notes of all your successful projects rather than try to gather this information just before your appraisal is due. If your boss disagrees with your assessment of your performance, you will have a few examples to illustrate how well you have achieved objectives.

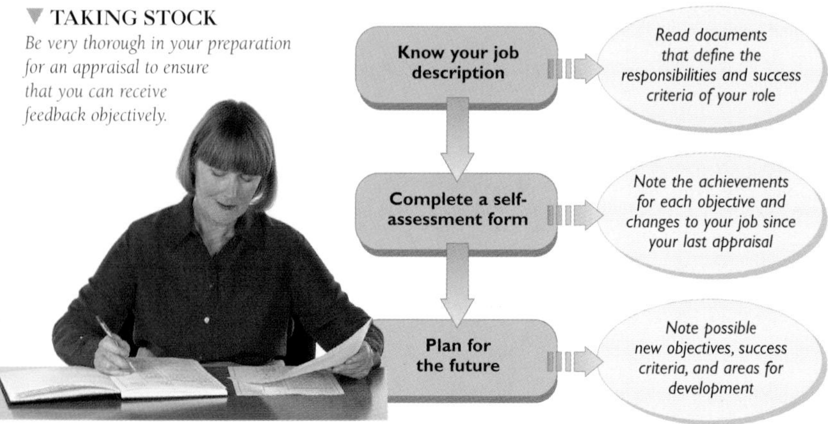

▼ **TAKING STOCK**
Be very thorough in your preparation for an appraisal to ensure that you can receive feedback objectively.

ACCEPTING RESPONSIBILITY

If you have not achieved all your objectives, accept responsibility for your own shortcomings, and take steps to improve your performance. If your boss does not give you sufficient feedback, ask him for his views on your work. Learn to handle all his feedback constructively, even if it is given in a demotivating manner. Because you have prepared beforehand, you will be able to evaluate whether or not the feedback is fair.

◀ **COPING WITH NEGATIVE FEEDBACK**
When you receive feedback, even if you do not agree with it, it is important to acknowledge the information about how someone else perceives you and your work, and learn from it.

SETTING OBJECTIVES

Even if you do not always get on with your boss, focusing on SMART objectives will minimize the likelihood of conflict. Have no more than six SMART objectives to focus on. Write out your objectives in specific language, using action words. Describe what you would see, hear, or feel when you have achieved each objective. These qualitative measures, described in your own words, increase your sense of involvement with your job. Achieving objectives will help to keep your commitment high, even if you are in contention with your boss.

61 Set demanding objectives that challenge you.

62 Measure your work both qualitatively and quantitatively.

MEETING SMART OBJECTIVES

SPECIFIC	Establish what you are meant to achieve—and when and how.
MEASURABLE	Define resources to be used and expected results using actual figures.
ACHIEVABLE	Suggest what is achievable and agree on this with your boss.
RELEVANT	Ensure objectives are challenging, yet within your capabilities and control.
TIME-BASED	Agree on the timescale for completion and the frequency of review.

TAKING CRITICISM

If you regard criticism as a means to help you improve, rather than a list of your failings to defend, you will be able to view your boss's feedback objectively and not take it personally. Listen to your boss's comments as if they were observations about someone else. If there is a discrepancy between your own and your boss's view of your performance, you may need to communicate more with your boss. If your boss is reluctant to give you feedback because she fears your reaction, ask her frequently how you can improve. It is better to receive comments about small problems as they arise than to receive all the criticism at once.

ACCEPTING PRAISE

Acknowledge praise from your boss without embarrassment. If you belittle or dismiss praise, you will receive it less often. A simple "thank you" is the best reply if you feel awkward about accepting praise. However, try to find out what exactly your boss appreciated about your work in order to get valuable and focused feedback.

RESPONDING POSITIVELY

When receiving feedback from your boss, keep your body language open and maintain eye contact. You may agree verbally, but your body language may contradict what you are saying.

NEGATIVE BODY LANGUAGE

POSITIVE BODY LANGUAGE

REACTING TO CRITICISM

It is seldom easy to listen to criticism, and your reaction to it depends on the tone of voice and manner in which it is given. In some ways, criticism is even more difficult to take if you accept that it is justified. Give yourself time to think by asking for specifics and taking the time you need to give a considered response:

"I need some time to think about what you said about my work."

"Which part of the report did you think would be confusing to the customer?"

"What would you like me to change about the way I approach my work?"

EVALUATING CRITICISM

If negative feedback comes from a number of sources, you need to assess the criticism. When your boss criticizes you, consider her viewpoint. If her views are too general to act upon, ask for examples to help you to understand what you need to improve. Explore with her when her impression was formed. Ask for feedback from people who work with or for you. In this way, you can assess common factors that other people, as well as your boss, have noticed, and decide what needs to change.

63 Always act on feedback from customers.

64 Give less weight to feedback from competitors.

65 Take notes during feedback sessions to avoid the risk of ambiguity.

PLANNING ACTION

Feedback sessions with your boss should result in action. If the discussion was intended to resolve an area of conflict, the issue will recur or remain unresolved if no preventive action is taken. After a formal appraisal, make an action plan or a personal development plan and highlight areas to be focused on, and deadlines by which certain objectives should be achieved. The plan should also list the ways in which your boss can help you to develop the skills you will need.

▼ **CREATING A PLAN**
Note down actions as they are agreed with your boss, with a summary at the end, so that you leave with a definite plan.

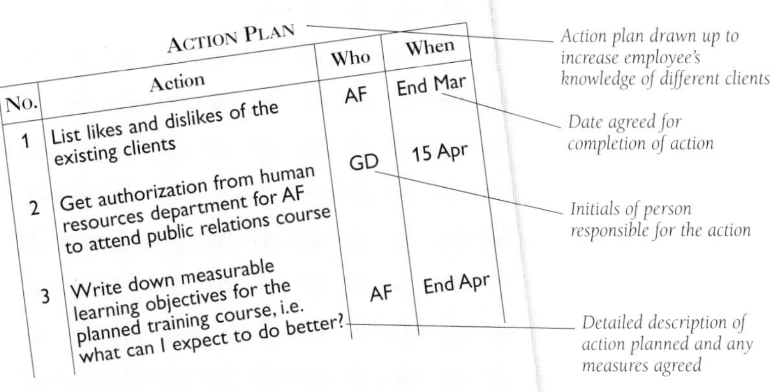

ACTION PLAN

No.	Action	Who	When
1	List likes and dislikes of the existing clients	AF	End Mar
2	Get authorization from human resources department for AF to attend public relations course	GD	15 Apr
3	Write down measurable learning objectives for the planned training course, i.e. what can I expect to do better?	AF	End Apr

TAKING THE INITIATIVE

Showing initiative without usurping your boss's role is a difficult balancing act. Be aware of your boss's reactions to your making decisions or offering suggestions, and acknowledge her help, so that she sees you as a supporter rather than as a competitor.

66 Ask how often your boss wants a review meeting or a report.

QUESTIONS TO ASK YOURSELF

- **Q** Do I know which outcomes are important to my boss?
- **Q** What resources and support can I draw on to achieve the expected results?
- **Q** Do I know what impact the project might have on the organization?
- **Q** Am I aware of any sensitivities or adverse consequences of taking on this work?

CLARIFYING THE BRIEF

Your boss may be happy that you are acting on your own initiative—as long as you reassure her that you are spending your time on the right things. When she briefs you on a new responsibility or project, find out the standards of performance she expects. Some bosses give a scant, rapid brief and you will need to ask questions to make sure you have fully understood what you are to do. Keep your boss informed about progress on key areas to ensure there is no difference of opinion later about what you should have done.

FLOATING SUGGESTIONS

Proposals that conflict with your boss's view may be more acceptable to her if you label them as suggestions. Your boss may not like being told what to do, but suggestions are acceptable since the decision is left open. Before you put forward your idea, outline the reasons behind it. This will tell your boss that she should listen to what you are about to say. If she has to guess at your motives, she may misinterpret your suggestion. If your boss proposes something that you disagree with, do not immediately make a countersuggestion, or she will think that you have not listened. Take time to consider her views and look for the elements you agree with.

CULTURAL DIFFERENCES

The extent to which you can take the initiative depends on your boss's style, and the organizational culture. In the US, a boss is likely to encourage independent action. In the UK, however, she will expect polite acknowledgment that she is the boss. In Japan, no step will be taken without the consensus of the whole team.

67 Show enthusiasm for achieving joint objectives.

BUILDING AND SUPPORTING

Always give credit to your boss just as you would expect her to credit you for your own work. In meetings, show your initiative and support for your boss simultaneously by building on what your boss has said or linking your suggestion with her earlier contribution. Never oppose your boss's known point of view in a meeting with others without her knowledge, even if she is not present. Your boss may get to hear of this and may curb your freedom to act on your own.

▼ **SHOWING SUPPORT**

When your boss is speaking, maintain eye contact and look interested. If your boss is facing opposition, show you agree with your boss and put forward the benefits you see in her suggestions.

Boss outlines plan of action

Team member backs up boss's proposal

Client's initial scepticism about the plan is dispelled

BEING DIPLOMATIC

As you become noticed in the organization, it is diplomatic to remember your boss's help when others are praising you for your achievements. Show your appreciation of your boss's support in your development, without diminishing your own contribution. Even though you may now be approached independently for advice, show respect for your boss—continue to ask rather than tell her what you will do next. Showing due deference while being assertive sends a message to your boss that you understand where your loyalty lies.

68 Be careful of what you say in your boss's absence.

69 Show your boss that you are not in competition.

PROTECTING YOURSELF

It is important to be seen as someone who delivers as promised, to avoid being blamed when things go wrong. What your boss needs during challenging times is not conflict but someone he can trust to handle important issues with no unpleasant surprises.

70 Ensure that you and your boss present a united front in a crisis.

71 Drop, delay, or delegate anything that is not urgent if you sense a crisis is imminent.

KEEPING THE RIGHT FOCUS

When things go wrong in organizations, people tend to look for a scapegoat, and you need to protect your reputation if you want to stay in your job. In a crisis, you and your boss may come under scrutiny, and it is essential to remain focused on what is important. Review your key goals. Often, 20 percent of your effort achieves 80 percent of the results—find out which objectives have the maximum effect. Then consider the publicity factor—which goals most enhance your and your boss's reputation if you succeed, or cause most embarrassment if you fail? Focus on these few key objectives to accelerate your impact on results.

72 Shut out any distractions in times of difficulty.

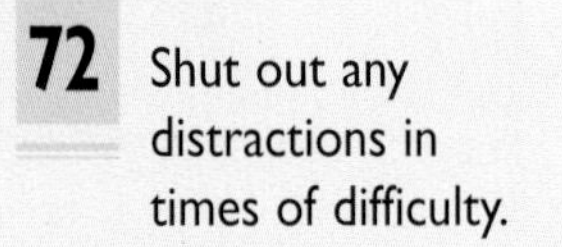

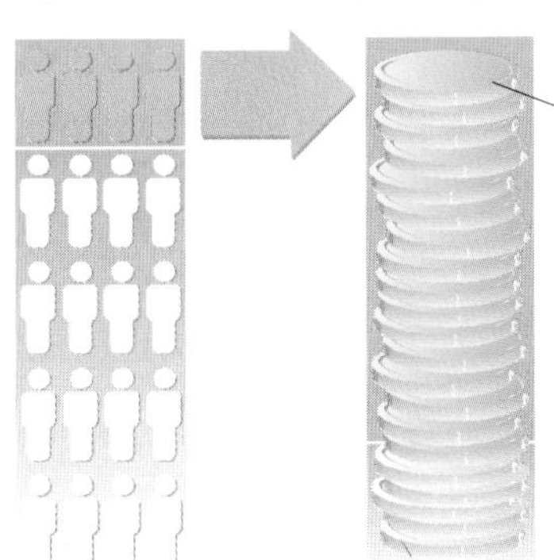

Over 80 percent of revenue comes from under 20 percent of customers, so your main focus should be that small proportion of customers

USING THE 80/20 RULE ▶
The 80/20 rule devised by Vilfredo Pareto states that a few causes are responsible for a large percentage of the effect. This can be applied to any number of situations—for example, to identify your key customers and prioritize your tasks accordingly.

BEING SEEN TO DELIVER

It is not enough to perform your job to a high standard if you and your boss are under threat. You should ensure that other people are aware of your success as a team. It is too late to have a publicity campaign when the downturn has started. You need to be working on this during the good times. Manage your own and your boss's chances of survival by focusing on your influential internal customers as well as external ones.

POINTS TO REMEMBER

- The blame for problems in organizations tends to fall on people who are seen to perform below required standards.
- You need to make people aware of your own and your boss's achievements.
- It is important to be prepared for unexpected problems.

73 Preempt problems with other people by sustaining good relationships.

GUARDING AGAINST THE UNEXPECTED

In a fast-moving business environment, there is always a risk that unforeseen problems will arise. Even if your boss trusts you to use your initiative and make decisions, keep him well-briefed—especially about anything unexpected. Anticipate conflicts that might arise with customers or colleagues in other departments. Guard against mistakes that you can avoid. Own up to more major problems, with proposed solutions, in time for them to be corrected.

▼ **AVOIDING SURPRISES**

Ensure that your boss and clients are never caught unawares by adverse information. Advise them of the problem before someone else does.

Team member puts forward a plan to tackle a potential problem

Boss is reassured that the clients' interests are being protected

DEALING WITH STRESS

Stress is often a sign of potential conflict that has not been dealt with. Being able to identify symptoms of stress in yourself or your boss will enable you to do something about the causes before stress becomes a problem that affects your work.

74 Talk over stressful situations with a friend before you talk to your boss.

75 Take relaxation breaks to relieve work pressure.

76 Spot the physical signs of unresolved emotional conflict.

RECOGNIZING SYMPTOMS

Being constantly late, forgetful, unable to make decisions, and unconcerned about personal appearance are behavioral symptoms of stress. Emotional symptoms include anger or fearfulness, and can lead to a withdrawal from relationships at work. The physical effects of stress, such as back or neck pain, or ulcers, often recur. Although all these could be due to unrelated problems, when you notice a number of symptoms simultaneously in yourself or your boss, stress is the likely cause.

IDENTIFYING CAUSES

Conflict in the workplace can cause stress and high levels of stress can cause conflict. Your boss may expect too much from you, leading to a deterioration in your relationship and the quality of your work. Or she may not allow you any control over schedules, or a say in decision-making—feeling undervalued and underused can prove to be equally stressful. If you feel that stress is affecting your performance and you are losing your perspective, raise the issue with your boss before the situation overwhelms you.

▲ **WORKING LATE**
Unpredictable working hours are a major cause of stress. Organize your tasks and your time to avoid having to work overtime continually.

MANAGING STRESS

If you feel constantly under pressure at work, you need to review how you manage and delegate work. You can do the same for your boss and make suggestions about how you could support, or be supported, to keep both of you as tension-free as possible. Long-term stress has an adverse effect on creativity, health, and performance, and all these can affect the profitability of an organization. Exercise regularly, adopt a well-balanced diet and eat at regular times, and get enough sleep to give yourself a chance to cope—even thrive—under pressure. Encourage your boss to maintain the same regime.

77 Recognize that you need some short-term stress to raise performance and tackle challenges.

▼ **GETTING AWAY**
When you are spending time with your family or friends, leave all work issues behind you. Your time off should rejuvenate you to face your routine tasks again.

▼ **BALANCING WORK AND LIFE**
Planning focuses your time on important goals. If you have a disorganized working style, you will spend this time reacting to crises rather than concentrating on your priorities.

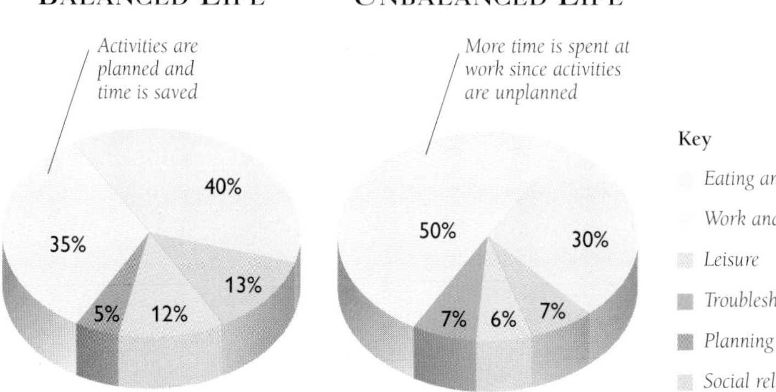

COPING WITH HARASSMENT

One of the most damaging forms of conflict at work can be harassment from your boss. In such a situation you need to state what you find unacceptable. If nothing changes, know your rights and how to protect yourself if you decide to complain.

78 Ask questions to ascertain if your boss's harassment is deliberate.

KNOWING YOUR RIGHTS

If you are being harassed by your boss, as a one-time incident or by being worn down through unkind or prejudiced comments, you have rights. In a one-on-one meeting, tell your boss how you feel about his behaviour. If he is sexually harassing you or making offensive racial remarks, tell him to stop. If you are being treated unfairly, remember there are employment laws against discrimination in the workplace, and human rights laws to preserve your dignity at work.

ASSERTIVE BILL OF RIGHTS

I have the right to:

- Be treated with respect
- Express my opinions and feelings
- Have my contribution listened to
- Ask for what I want and need
- Express my beliefs
- Say "no" without feeling guilty
- Make mistakes as part of gaining experience
- Choose how I behave and take the consequences
- Receive reasonable notice of changes to my job
- Work in an environment that is not damaging to me

◀ **SETTING THE LIMITS**

Remembering these guidelines will help you realize when your boss has overstepped the boundaries. These rights bring with them the responsibility to afford the same rights to others.

PREPARING YOUR CASE

If your boss's behavior is upsetting you, keep a log of events and prepare to present your case to someone else for help. Record the date and time of every incident, anyone else observing or involved, and what action you took. Keep copies of any correspondence or notes of relevant conversations. Prepare to follow the grievance procedure of your organization—this will entail making a complaint in writing to senior management and will likely involve the human resources department.

79 Assess the impact of your boss's behavior on you.

80 Ensure you have a network of people to support you.

TAKING ACTION

If, having spoken to your boss, the unacceptable behavior continues, approach someone else. Get outside advice, if this is free of charge, before you ask for internal help. Talk in confidence to unions, government-funded or other agencies, or lawyers, who advise citizens on their legal rights and can help you with your case. If an assault is involved or you are forced to leave your job unfairly, this could involve legal action. Accept help to cope with the likely consequences, both legal and emotional.

DECIDING TO LEAVE

A bullying boss can erode your self-esteem, attack your self-confidence, and leave you afraid of the next humiliating experience. You have to decide whether the job is worth the personal costs. Consider if there is any future for the working relationship. Support within the organization from colleagues, personnel, or senior management can alleviate the situation. If you do not receive inside support, you may have no choice but to leave.

▲ **SEEKING LEGAL HELP**
Get legal advice before resigning to find out if you are eligible for compensation for constructive dismissal.

STANDING YOUR GROUND ▶
Sally got used to her boss's criticism and blamed herself instead of insisting her boss treat her fairly. Help from a colleague, her follow-up action, and her boss's change of behavior, saved her from further psychological suffering. Her boss was also spared from legal action for harassment and bullying.

CASE STUDY

Nothing Sally did was ever good enough for her boss. When Sally asked what she could do to improve her work, he would dismissively say that he had no time to go through her long list of mistakes. Gradually Sally lost confidence and spent many unproductive hours trying to correct her work on her own. A new employee joined work and he was much more assertive with the boss. He told Sally their boss had no right to cause her such distress and suggested she ask him for specific feedback. In a meeting, with her boss, Sally stated how upset she was that her work was not valued and described how she felt their relationship could be improved. Her boss was surprised by the feedback and apologized for being impatient under stress. Over time he realized he could rely on his team for effective help without bullying them.

IMPROVING YOUR PROSPECTS

Your boss can help you gain the skills you need to achieve a better salary package and promotion. Take on more responsibility in your job and gain your boss's agreement to your career plans.

EXPANDING YOUR ROLE

It would be surprising if your role at work remained unchanged between annual reviews. There will always be new aspects of your job with potential for growth and gaining experience. It is up to you to make the best of these opportunities.

82 Recall a challenge you have overcome and use it to learn about yourself.

83 Record what has changed in your role and why.

POINTS TO REMEMBER

- The success of long-term goals should be periodically assessed.
- The latest professional trends need to be kept in mind.
- Self-development should not be neglected or postponed.

REVIEWING YOURSELF

Your appraisal is a formal opportunity to review, with your boss, the changes in your role, and to record these as a revised job description. However, you should also review your own progress independently of your boss and update your resume at least once a year. Reflect on the new skills you have acquired and strengths you have shown. Identify aspects of your performance that could improve. Note the changes over the last year and anticipate the likely changes in the next year. Continuous improvement is essential in any role—if nothing has changed, you have a problem.

FOCUSING ON AREAS OF GROWTH

By reflecting on what has changed in your role, you can focus on areas for development in discussions with your boss. Any expansion of your organization is your best chance for proving yourself. Ask your boss questions about any new initiatives the organization may be planning. Do some research on whether outside trends favor the changes proposed. Ask yourself what impact the new direction will have on your future role. If you see a real opportunity for growth in a new area, volunteer, with your boss's support, to work on associated projects to get yourself noticed.

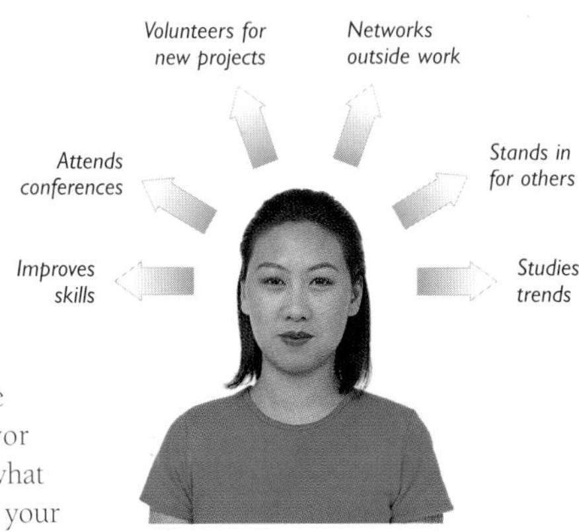

▲ **EXPANDING HORIZONS**
It is essential to capitalize on as many growth opportunities as possible, within and outside the organization, to expand your role.

GAINING EXPERIENCE

In a flat organizational structure, promotion could be slower than you would like. Discuss with your boss how to gain the experience and skills you will need to be promoted. For example, could you do this through special projects, redeployment to another area or an associated organization, or by standing in for someone in a more senior position while they are away? As you build trust with your boss, you can persuade her to delegate more and more responsibility to you. Deputizing for her when she is away becomes a natural next step. Offer to attend conferences and report back to colleagues on what you have learned that will be useful to the organization.

◀ **MAKING THE MOST OF CONTACTS**
In your own time, network with people involved in some way with your work. Build up a contact list of people who can keep you updated on professional developments or who may become customers in the future.

LEADING FROM BEHIND

If your boss's performance is standing still, you are both going backward in real terms. Show leadership by continuously improving your own and your boss's skills and supporting your boss while at the same time retaining visibility yourself.

84 Help your boss recognize that change is taking place at work.

85 Link suggestions for improvement with profitability.

86 Look for suitable mentors for you and your boss.

SUGGESTING CHANGES

In a learning organization, suggesting new ways to do things is a natural way of life. Review performance improvements you have observed with your boss and the benefits to the organization in terms of business objectives achieved. Your suggestions will be more acceptable if you link improvements to the increased satisfaction of customers, employees, and shareholders. Other relevant objectives might be revenue increases, cost and time savings, and avoiding waste.

▼ **LEARNING TO GROW**
A learning organization is constantly looking for ways in which it can develop and improve its performance.

87 Suggest hiring research students to inject new ideas.

DEVELOPING YOUR BOSS

Your boss may have amassed experience over the years but like everyone, she needs to improve continuously and keep her knowledge updated. As you discuss your development with your boss, you can encourage her to consider appropriate activities for herself. If you have discovered interesting network groups, introduce your boss to your contacts or, with her permission, suggest her as a conference speaker. Keep her abreast of research or vital information on other organizations relevant to new initiatives she is working on.

▼ **HELPING YOUR BOSS KEEP UP TO DATE**

Encourage your boss to attend meetings on relevant topics arranged by membership organizations for managers and directors to gather ideas to try out at work.

Manager contributes an idea for networking group to improve sales

Senior manager explains how she achieves results

New manager jots down key learning points

RETAINING VISIBILITY

To lead from behind successfully, you will have to resign yourself to your boss gaining glory from your joint achievements. A fair boss will tell others about your contribution. In informal conversation, assess how visible you are to other departments or senior management. Put your name on reports you write and observe whether your boss leaves this information on copies sent to others. Suggest ways in which you can represent your organization to retain visibility without antagonizing your boss.

THINGS TO DO

1. Check informally if others know of your contribution.
2. Include the names of those responsible for new ideas in minutes of meetings.
3. Participate in networking or action groups.

FINDING HELP WITH SELF-DEVELOPMENT

Identify your development needs and suggest to your boss the activities and training that will help you most. You can persuade your boss to invest in your future and make yourself more marketable by presenting the benefits for both of you.

88 Think long term if you wish to progress higher in the organization.

89 Manage yourself first to have time to manage others well.

IDENTIFYING YOUR NEEDS

Look at your present performance and the skills you might need in a future job to identify your areas for development. Ask your boss what skills she thinks are needed for a job at the next level. As you rise higher, you will be judged on your people skills and how effectively you manage resources. How well do you manage people? Can you set up and lead teams? How adept are you at long-term strategic thinking—an essential skill if you want to progress higher in the organization?

CASE STUDY

Pablo Garcia had received feedback in his appraisal that his interpersonal skills needed to be developed. As suggested, he attended a workshop on communication skills. During the training, Pablo watched a video recording of himself talking with a colleague and was able to observe that his body language conveyed the opposite of enthusiasm.

At the next team meeting, when Pablo had to present a new idea to the team, he made a point of maintaining eye contact with the whole team and varying the tone of his voice. He then asked questions to gain feedback and looked interested in the team's reaction. Impressed by the clear presentation, his colleagues supported his ideas for the new project. Seeing his success at winning the team over, his boss congratulated him and made a mental note to put his name forward for a promotion.

◀ WORKING ON YOUR WEAKNESSES
In this example, an employee made full use of a self-development course to earn praise from his boss and colleagues, and improve his chances of promotion.

UNDERSTANDING THE THREE TYPES OF TRAINING

PRINCIPLES	PEOPLE	PROCESSES
Business Management	Career Counseling	Critical Thinking
Finance	Coaching	Problem-solving
Health & Safety	Delegation	Process Management
Marketing	Facilitation	Project Management
Selling	Leadership	Strategic Management
Technical or Technological	Recruitment & Selection	Time Management

PLANNING DEVELOPMENT ACTIVITIES

Work out with your boss the optimum timing and type of development activities to meet your needs. There are many ways, in addition to formal courses, to achieve personal growth. Set yourself a target of reading two management books per month on the areas you need to develop. Play tapes on management topics while you commute. Ask your boss to hire management videos that employees can watch at lunchtime. Note the key points you have learned, and put them into practice.

90 Listen to audio cassettes of self-help books.

91 Think laterally about how to gain self-development.

▲ LEARNING TOGETHER
Meet with colleagues occasionally to share the self-development techniques you have learned, and try to make them part of your routine.

LOOKING AHEAD

Reassure your boss that your organization will gain a return for the expense incurred by it on your self-development. A lengthy course at a business school, for example, is a large investment by any employer. Your organization may insist that you remain an employee for some time beyond course completion, so that you can apply your newly gained skills to your work. Apart from relying on your employer, find ways to undertake self-development in your own time, to improve your prospects for promotion.

GAINING AGREEMENT

If you want your boss to agree to something you propose, choose your moment carefully. Present the benefits well—especially if you are requesting a promotion or transfer, or an investment in your development—to make it easy for him to say "yes."

92 Check your boss's schedule to ensure he can give you his full attention.

QUESTIONS TO ASK YOURSELF

Q Is my proposal concise and easy to assimilate?

Q Is my case convincing as a business proposition?

Q At what time of the day does my boss function the best?

Q Is my boss under particular pressure from some other work at the moment?

Q Is my boss expressing real concerns I need to reassure him about, or just excuses?

CHOOSING YOUR MOMENT

Be sensitive to times when your boss is under pressure, but do not put off important issues indefinitely. If your boss agrees with your proposal, you will probably get an immediate response. Delay usually means there was something wrong with your proposal, unless your boss has been out of the office or is occupied on a particular project. Note your boss's designated times for going through his in-tray, making phone calls, or when his open door indicates that you can interrupt. Observe whether he prefers to meet team members early in the morning or later in the day.

Employee has adequate time to explain her plan clearly

▼ **TIMING IT RIGHT**
Choose the time when your boss is most receptive if you want an affirmative response to your proposal.

PRESENTING THE BENEFITS

Think of the benefits of your proposal from your boss's perspective—as an individual, leader of your team, and as a representative of the organization. A boss with a financial background will want to make sure you have prepared a realistic and cost-conscious budget for your proposal. If your boss is a people person, your benefits should relate to satisfaction, motivation, and teamwork. Describe how your performance will improve, if your proposal is accepted, in terms that match your boss's way of thinking.

93 List the benefits of your proposal succinctly.

94 Review all the factors that will affect your plan

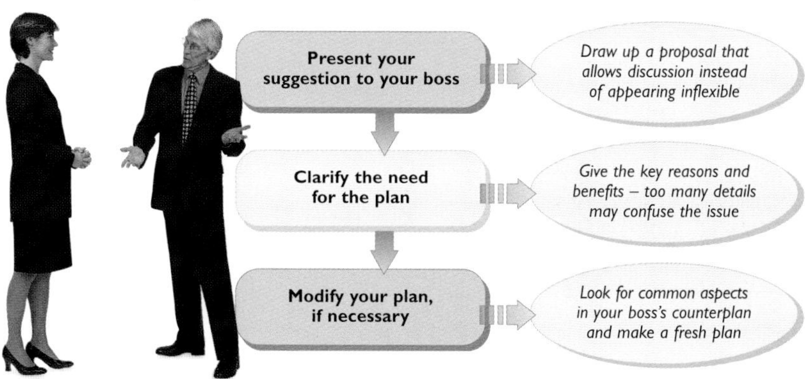

▲ PREPARING A FLEXIBLE PLAN

Do your research well before you present your plan so that you can counter your boss's objections, or make adjustments to your plan where necessary.

95 Ask questions to assess your boss's reaction to your proposed plan.

MAKING "YES" THE EASY OPTION

Present a well-thought-out, logical plan and make it hard for your boss to refuse. If your boss hesitates to give his approval, keep questioning him until you understand his reservations. Make sure these are legitimate concerns rather than delaying tactics. Attempt to overcome your boss's concerns by presenting the benefits and ask for his agreement. If at this point, you still receive a negative reply, ask what it is that is still not quite right. Persistence should pay off in the end.

NEGOTIATING A RAISE

Most people will accept a salary that is not the highest available for the job, as long as the amount feels fair as an indication of their worth. Assess your value to the organization and present a case for a raise, based on the value you have added.

96 Make your case for a raise factually, assertively, and persistently.

▲ **BEING SURE OF YOUR WORTH**

Asking your boss for a raise does not imply disloyalty to him. Overcome such misconceptions by confidently presenting your arguments for a higher salary.

VALUING YOURSELF

You may feel uncomfortable asking your boss for more money. However, if you think that you are no longer receiving the appropriate pay for the job you are doing, you need to ask for a raise to show that you value yourself. You may be the type of person who focuses on doing a good job and would be happy to take a promotion based on job title rather than money—but you need to make sure you are not being taken for granted. Research salaries for the same kind of job in your own or another organization to ensure that you are proposing a fair salary, before you approach your boss.

DOS AND DON'TS

- ✔ Do be sure of your major objective.
- ✔ Do outline the elements of your package that you would like to improve.
- ✔ Do concede on the items of least importance to you.
- ✔ Do confirm what was agreed upon.
- ✔ Do present options so your boss has a choice.

- ✗ Don't lose focus on your key objective.
- ✗ Don't be so swayed by your boss's point of view that you fail to present your case well.
- ✗ Don't concede to your boss's modifications right away.
- ✗ Don't get emotional if you are turned down.
- ✗ Don't present a case unsupported by facts.

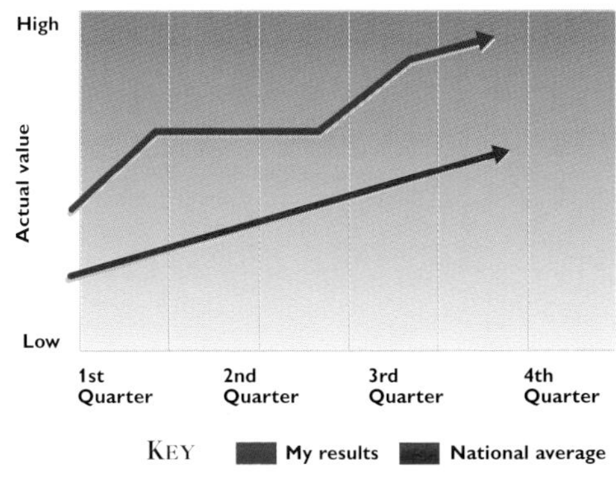

▲ TOTALLING UP THE BALANCE
Prepare a record of your successes. Put an actual value, such as revenue generated or number of hours saved, against each entry to convince your boss that you deserve a raise.

SHOWING HOW YOU ADD VALUE

If you focus on your personal needs when you ask for a raise, you are unlikely to meet with a positive response. Present a good case based on the extra responsibilities that you have taken on, money that you have saved or earned for your organization, or additional skills you are applying to save time and improve quality. Drawing up a value-added business case is most likely to gain the consideration of your boss.

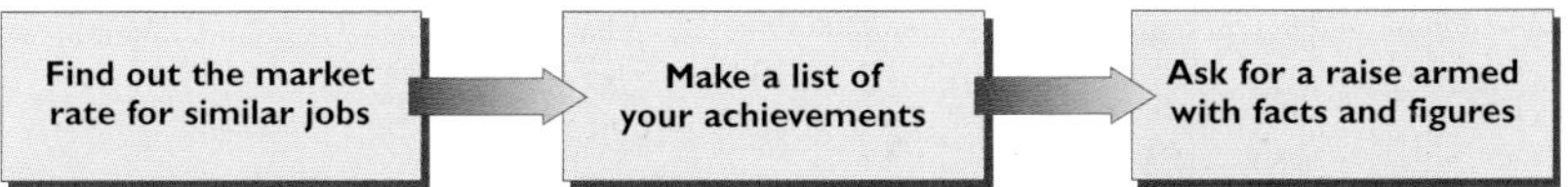

▲ BEING PREPARED
You can confidently ask your boss for a raise if you do your research well and have all the relevant information in place.

MAKING IT HAPPEN

When you are convinced about your added-value business case, ask your boss for a one-on-one meeting. Calm, persistent repetition of your request is the right approach. If your boss raises objections, explain why you think the salary range you are asking for is right. If your boss thinks you do not deserve a pay raise, despite your business case, ask him what else you would need to do. If your boss tells you that his hands are tied as he has budget constraints, the minimum you should ask for is a review within six months. Follow up this discussion with a memo mentioning the date agreed upon and thanking him—it will be useful to refer to later if he needs reminding of his promise.

POINTS TO REMEMBER

- You need to believe in your own worth and in the value you add to the organization.
- An increase in your salary will often entail an increase in responsibilities or workload.
- The benefits of what you suggest should be outlined to your boss.
- Your boss should be made aware of your achievements.

GETTING A PROMOTION

Your boss has a direct influence on your chances of promotion. Make it clear to her that you are ready for promotion by behaving as if you are already at the next level. She may even offer help on external promotion if you have been open with her.

97 Always advise your boss before you apply for an internal promotion.

98 Keep your boss updated about your career goals.

99 Ask your boss if you are ready for promotion.

MANAGING YOUR PROMOTION

Your organization's appraisal program may require your boss to discuss career paths with you. Review your opportunities for internal promotion with your boss at appraisal time and ask her to help in facilitating the transition. If you plan to apply within the organization, discuss it with your boss first. She will be a key referee for both internal and external applications. Assess the new skills you have acquired with her and review how they will help in your transfer to your new position.

BEHAVING AS IF PROMOTED

If your boss is a good role-model, you should already be clear on how to behave at the next level. Observe who is valued in your workplace and for what skills and personal qualities. If working long hours appears to be the common factor for being promoted, consider if this is what you really want. Initiative, creativity, or good people skills may be the criteria you need to emulate. Network with people who could be useful when you are promoted.

Friendly contact gives tips on job

GAINING THE SUPPORT OF OTHERS

Do not worry about taking up the time of people who could help you up the career ladder. Turn your boss and colleagues into advocates for you.

BE READY
With your people skills in place, you are ready for a more responsible role.

INTERACT WITH YOUR BOSS
Use listening and questioning skills to learn from your boss.

HELP OTHERS
Develop your management skills by investing time in the talents of those who work with you.

MANAGE INDIRECTLY
Recognize the larger team that you work with outside your work group and use your influencing skills.

START NOW
Even if you do not have a large team to practice on, you can start working on developing the leadership skills that you need for your future promotion.

Makes use of transferable skills to climb the corporate ladder

◀ **TRANSFERRING SKILLS**
Take advantage of every opportunity to polish your skills to make the transition to a higher-level job smooth and trouble-free.

HONING YOUR SKILLS

Listen carefully to feedback about the competencies needed for a promotion—from your boss and others whose opinion you value—and start working on them. Your time and resource management talents and leadership skills need to match the level above you. Count how many relationships with colleagues, contractors, and suppliers you have to manage. You probably have influence over a larger number of people than you directly manage. One way to improve your management skills is to volunteer as a mentor to others.

POINTS TO REMEMBER

- Your behavior should match that of people at the next level.
- You may sometimes need to make it clear to your boss that you are ready for promotion.
- It is important to discuss your career goals in general terms with contacts outside the office.
- You need to ask your boss how to be selected for promotion and make a good start in the new role.

PREPARING FOR CHANGE

Find out who has been successfully promoted in the organization and note any common factors. Ask what was most difficult and most easy about the transition. If your boss supports your case for promotion, ask her whether she agrees with your assessment of how you meet the criteria for the new job. Recognize her contribution to your readiness for promotion and consider how you could minimize disruption when you move on. Think about how you could help your boss in finding a successor.

THINGS TO DO

1. Ask your boss what qualities you need to be promoted to her level.
2. Ask her how she would deal with issues in the new job.
3. See if any of your team members can be promoted to take your place.

Well-prepared candidate faces panel with confidence

BEING INTERVIEWED

Try to find out who else is competing for the promotion. Assess their strengths and weaknesses and look at the same for yourself. Never assume that the interviewer will know about your past achievements, whether you are an internal or external candidate. This is not the time to be modest—you need to state what your strengths are and cite successful projects.

◀ HANDLING INTERVIEWS

Be prepared for a one-on-one interview, a panel interview, group sessions, or an interview at an assessment center for the selection process.

KNOWING THE LIKELY QUESTIONS

WHAT YOU ASK

- What major challenges do you anticipate in the next year?
- What are the key success factors in this job?
- What qualities are you looking for in the person who does this job?
- What opportunities are there to gain further development or qualifications?

WHAT YOU ARE ASKED

- What has presented the greatest challenge to you in the last two years?
- What are your strengths and weaknesses?
- What has been the most valuable thing you have learned in your current job?
- What training and development would you need to do this job?

PLANNING FOR SUCCESS

You should devise an outline plan for what you would do in your first few months of the new job. You may be asked about this at your interview to see if you have really understood what is involved. Talk to your boss and anyone who knows the new department or organization you are joining. Read any relevant reports, articles, or publicity. Find out what your predecessor was like, how much of a change you will be to your new team, and how are they performing currently. Assess who will be your new allies. If you can, plan to take a vacation before starting your new job. Use this time to relax and also to think through exactly how you will make a good impression with your new team, your new colleagues, and your new boss.

100 Prepare your own questions to ask at interviews.

101 Set yourself new and challenging goals to achieve in your new job.

▼ CELEBRATING SUCCESS
Celebrate your hard-earned promotion with all those who have been instrumental, directly or indirectly, in the achievement.

ASSESSING YOUR ABILITY

Test how well you are able to manage your boss and whether you have succeeded in turning your boss into your greatest advocate. Answer the following questions honestly. If your answer is "Never" mark option 1; if it is "Always" mark option 4 and so on. Add your scores together, and refer to the analysis at the end to see how you have scored. Use your answers to identify areas that need improvement.

OPTIONS

1 Never

2 Occasionally

3 Frequently

4 Always

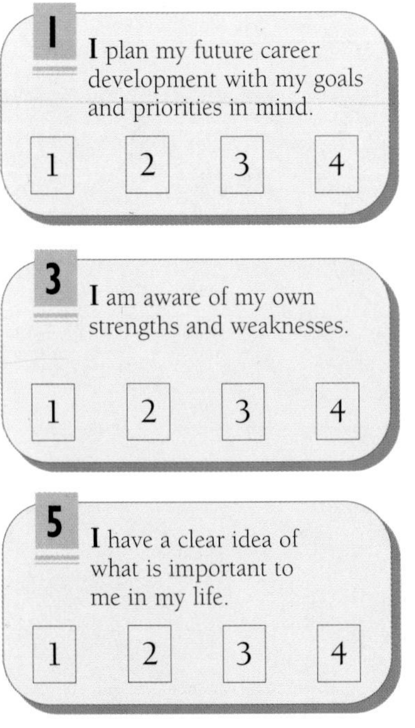

1 I plan my future career development with my goals and priorities in mind.

1 2 3 4

3 I am aware of my own strengths and weaknesses.

1 2 3 4

5 I have a clear idea of what is important to me in my life.

1 2 3 4

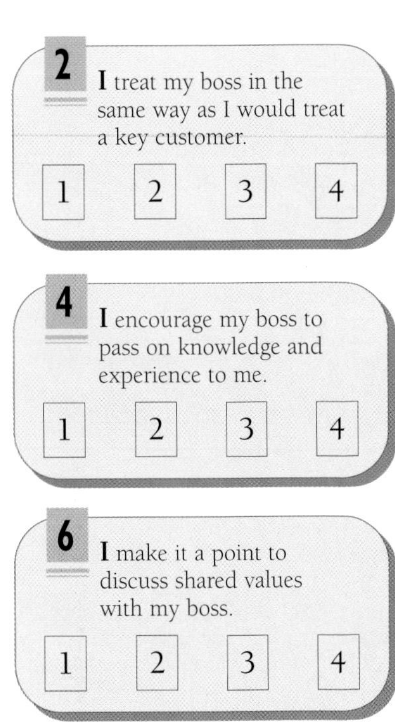

2 I treat my boss in the same way as I would treat a key customer.

1 2 3 4

4 I encourage my boss to pass on knowledge and experience to me.

1 2 3 4

6 I make it a point to discuss shared values with my boss.

1 2 3 4

7 **I** set objectives for what I wish for in different areas of my life.

1 2 3 4

8 **I** observe how people think in different ways.

1 2 3 4

9 **I** manage my work-life balance in my day-to-day routine.

1 2 3 4

10 **I** am able to say "No" assertively when necessary.

1 2 3 4

11 **I** encourage my boss and colleagues to give me feedback.

1 2 3 4

12 **I** keep my boss updated on the progress of projects I am working on.

1 2 3 4

13 **I** observe and assess my boss's strengths and weaknesses.

1 2 3 4

14 **I** make sure that I understand exactly what is expected of me.

1 2 3 4

15 **I** am assertive with my boss rather than passive or aggressive.

1 2 3 4

16 **I** encourage my boss to delegate responsibility and authority to me.

1 2 3 4

17 I listen carefully to my boss to identify any potential problems

1 2 3 4

18 I review my workload and discuss priorities with my boss.

1 2 3 4

19 I give my boss positive feedback about our achievements.

1 2 3 4

20 I make suggestions for change that my boss is happy to accept.

1 2 3 4

21 I pick the best time to discuss difficult issues with my boss.

1 2 3 4

22 I know how to create a good impression with my boss.

1 2 3 4

23 I present my boss with solutions, not problems.

1 2 3 4

24 I make sure my boss knows about any problems before anyone else.

1 2 3 4

25 I give constructive feedback on my boss's working style.

1 2 3 4

26 I present information in the way my boss prefers.

1 2 3 4

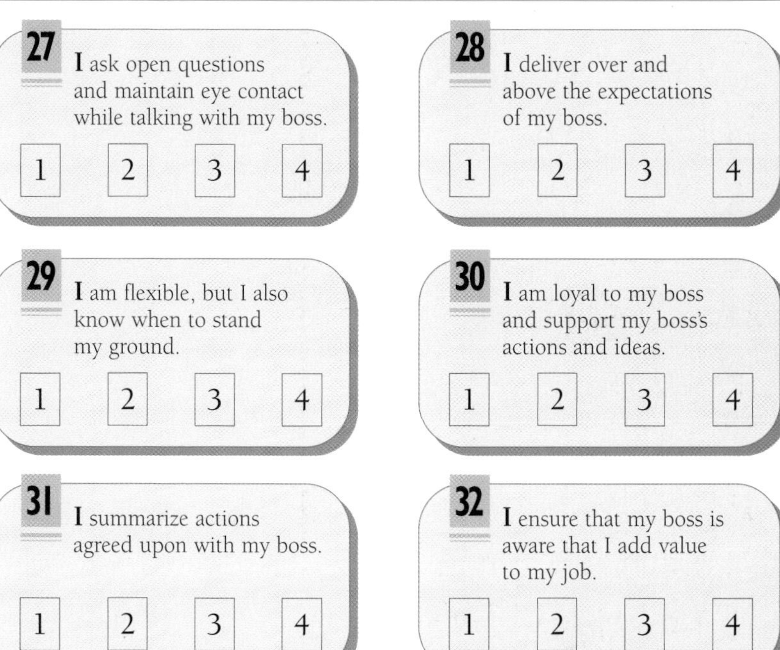

27 I ask open questions and maintain eye contact while talking with my boss.

1 2 3 4

28 I deliver over and above the expectations of my boss.

1 2 3 4

29 I am flexible, but I also know when to stand my ground.

1 2 3 4

30 I am loyal to my boss and support my boss's actions and ideas.

1 2 3 4

31 I summarize actions agreed upon with my boss.

1 2 3 4

32 I ensure that my boss is aware that I add value to my job.

1 2 3 4

ANALYSIS

Now that you have completed the self-assessment, add up your total score and check your performance. Whatever level of success you have achieved, there is always room for development. Identify your weakest areas, then refer back to the relevant sections of this book.

32–63: You need to be more proactive in managing your boss. Try and understand your boss's style of working. Be clear on objectives before you discuss them.

64–95: You are largely aware of how to manage your boss. Practice being more assertive and identify areas for self-development.

96–128: You are adept at managing your boss. Continuously develop yourself by asking for feedback and reviewing what you have learned.

INDEX

ACKNOWLEDGMENTS

AUTHOR'S ACKNOWLEDGMENTS

I would like to thank everyone who helped on this book, including Nicola Munro, Adèle Hayward, and Karen Self at DK London, and the DK team in New Delhi.

PUBLISHER'S ACKNOWLEDGMENTS

Dorling Kindersley would like to thank the following for their help and participation in producing this book:

Picture research Kavita Dutta
Picture librarian Richard Dabb
Indexer Margaret McCormack
Photography Gary Ombler, Steve Gorton, Mathew Ward, Andy Crawford, Tim Ridley

PICTURE CREDITS

Key: *a* above, *b* bottom, *c* center, *l* left, *r* right, *t* top
Corbis: Tom Stewart 4c; Jon Feingersh 7; Yang Liu 36; Michael Keller 49; Darama 53bl and 65; Raoul Minsart 57.
Stone/Getty Images: 48cl; **Superstock:** 21bl

AUTHOR'S BIOGRAPHY

Christina Osborne is Chief Executive of the strategic human resources consultancy Business Solutions, www.BSol.co.uk. Christina advises clients, ranging from entrepreneurs to multinationals, on designing organizations and developing people to succeed. Her roles as executive director have spanned personnel, marketing, and strategic planning, including mergers and acquisitions. Christina has held nonexecutive board roles in both public and private sectors and been engaged as a speaker on human resource strategy and as a mentor to chief executives and directors leading organizational change. Her wealth of experience on organizational strategy has confirmed the importance of executives learning how to manage their boss, especially in times of change. Christina is a Fellow of both the Chartered Institute of Personnel and Development and the Chartered Institute of Directors. She is author of *Appraising Staff* and *Dealing with Difficult People* in the Essential Managers series.

"Who's Joey?"

For several long moments, Jack didn't say anything. Alana was afraid he might not tell her. For reasons she didn't understand, it was suddenly critical that she know.

"Joey's the baby you gave birth to eight months ago," Jack informed her.

"W-what?"

Jack leaned in and got right in her face. "Joey's the little boy you abandoned." He stabbed his index finger at her. "And if you think you can get him back after all this time, think again. Joey is mine."

And with those words, Alana's entire life changed.

DELORES FOSSEN

SECRET DELIVERY

TORONTO NEW YORK LONDON
AMSTERDAM PARIS SYDNEY HAMBURG
STOCKHOLM ATHENS TOKYO MILAN MADRID
PRAGUE WARSAW BUDAPEST AUCKLAND

Recycling programs for this product may not exist in your area.

ISBN-13: 978-0-373-36548-7

SECRET DELIVERY

This edition published by arrangement with Harlequin Books S.A.

www.Harlequin.com

Printed in U.S.A.

ABOUT THE AUTHOR

Imagine a family tree that includes Texas cowboys, Choctaw and Cherokee Indians, a Louisiana pirate and a Scottish rebel who battled side by side with William Wallace. With ancestors like that, it's easy to understand why Texas author and former air force captain Delores Fossen feels as if she were genetically predisposed to writing romances. Along the way to fulfilling her DNA destiny, Delores married an air force top gun who just happens to be of Viking descent. With all those romantic bases covered, she doesn't have to look too far for inspiration.

Books by Delores Fossen

HARLEQUIN INTRIGUE

990—UNDERCOVER DADDY*
1008—STORK ALERT*
1026—THE CHRISTMAS CLUE*
1044—NEWBORN CONSPIRACY*
1050—THE HORSEMAN'S SON*
1075—QUESTIONING THE HEIRESS
1091—SECURITY BLANKET**
1110—BRANDED BY THE SHERIFF†
1116—EXPECTING TROUBLE†
1122—SECRET DELIVERY†

*Five-Alarm Babies
**Texas Paternity
†Texas Paternity: Boots and Booties

CAST OF CHARACTERS

Sheriff Jack Whitley—This small-town cowboy cop rescues a pregnant Alana Davis when her car plunges into a frozen creek. When Alana delivers the child and then disappears, Jack becomes guardian to her newborn, and he's none too happy about giving up the little boy when Alana makes a surprise return eight months later.

Alana Davis—Her broken memories have left her not knowing whom to trust. She goes to Jack, the hot Texas sheriff who's but a glimmer in her memory, and learns he's raising her son…and that a killer is after all three of them.

Joey Whitley—The baby Jack has raised as his own and the child Alana wants back.

Dr. Keith Bartolo—He delivered Joey and was one of the last people to see Alana before she mysteriously disappeared.

Ted Moore—Security guard who might have held Alana against her will.

Margaret Vargas—The nurse who participated in Alana's incarceration. Is she merely a pawn, or the mastermind behind the plot to kill Alana?

Sean Davis—Alana's brother. He's profited from his sister's absence but claims he's innocent and is only acting in Alana's best interest.

Parker Howell—The FBI agent who tried to set up the deal that ultimately led to Alana being in danger.

Eldon Thatcher—The assassin who wants Alana and Jack dead, and he's willing to use Joey to get to them.

Prologue

Willow Ridge, Texas

Sheriff Jack Whitley figured he had three minutes, maybe less, to save the woman's life.

He slammed on his brakes, and his Ford pickup skidded to a stop just inches from what was left of the bridge's ice-scabbed guardrail. Seconds earlier, a car had broken through the metal and plunged over the side. Since he'd been traveling from the opposite direction, he'd caught just a glimpse of terror on the driver's face before Mill's Creek had swallowed her and her car.

There was no time to remove his gun or shoes. No time to call for help. He grabbed the life hammer from his glove compartment, barreled out of his truck and, running, he dived right into the cold dark water.

Hell. He couldn't see. The creek was thick with winter silt that concealed just about everything, but he went on instinct. At the speed the woman was traveling when she slammed through the guardrail, she was probably thirty, maybe forty feet out. He surfaced only long enough to drag in a deep breath so he could go down after her again.

Seconds ticked off in his head, each one a frantic reminder that he had to get to her. He had to save her. *Now*. No one, not even he, could last long in this frozen water.

He ignored the numbing cold that was starting to smother him and focused, finally spotting her black Lexus angled nose-down with the headlights and front fender already sinking into the clots of mud on the creek floor.

Jack fought through the water to get to her. She was there, behind the steering wheel, her light-colored coat billowing around her like a ghost. Her eyes were closed. Maybe she was unconscious.

Or already dead.

He pushed that possibility aside and latched on to the door handle.

It was jammed.

Cursing to himself, he bashed the life hammer against the window. The sharp metal head of the emergency tool made a large enough hole so he could reach in, open the door and undo her seat belt.

The woman spilled into his arms.

He grabbed her and began to haul her to the surface. Each inch was a struggle. His lungs burned now, and his muscles began to knot. Somehow, though, he broke through the water and breathed in some much needed air, while the woman lay limp and lifeless in his arms.

Jack dragged her to the muddy embankment, tilted back her head and started mouth-to-mouth resuscitation. He literally gave her what little breath he had left.

Her eyes fluttered open. She coughed. And Jack said a very sincere prayer of thanks.

"We got lucky," he gasped.

She opened her mouth, but didn't speak. Her stark-blue eyes widened, and the sound she made was one of raw agony.

"What's wrong? Are you hurt?" Jack asked.

She didn't answer. She fought with her coat, shoving it open and clamping her hands over her belly.

Jack saw then that she was pregnant. She had to be in her last trimester.

"Help me. I'm in trouble." She looked up at him, her eyes shimmering with tears, her face twisted in pain. "*Please*. Don't let my baby die."

Her words slammed into him. They'd dodged one bullet, but another was headed right at them.

Jack scooped her into his arms and ran like hell toward his truck.

Chapter One

Eight months later

Alana Davis checked the rearview mirror again. The dark-colored car was still following her.

"Oh, God," she mumbled.

It couldn't be the security guard. It just couldn't be. Because if he'd managed to catch up with her, Alana figured this time he would kill her.

She couldn't stop, not even to find a pay phone and call the police. Not that there'd been a pay phone anywhere along the way from the secluded house in the woods where she'd been held captive. Nor was there one along the highway that had taken her nearly an hour to find. Luckily, the car she'd stolen from the front of the house had nearly a full tank of gas.

And thankfully, she'd seen the sign to the town of Willow Ridge.

The guard and a nurse had force-fed her a partial dose of sedatives only hours earlier, so it'd taken Alana a while to fight through dizziness and make the connection. Willow Ridge was just one of those floating memories that she couldn't immediately link to anything or anyone. But then she remembered Jack Whitley, the town's sheriff. He'd helped her.

She couldn't remember what he'd done exactly, but she instinctively knew she could trust him.

Alana couldn't say that about anyone else.

She certainly couldn't trust the guard or nurse. Or her brother. In fact, one of them must have been responsible for her captivity.

But which one?

And why?

She didn't know the answer to either question, but Jack Whitley would be able to find out.

Lightning rifled through the night sky. A few seconds later, thunder came, a thick rumbling groan. Shivering, she made the final turn that would take her to Willow Ridge. Even with the rain and her spotty vision, she could see the other vehicle make the turn right along behind her. He stayed close. Too close.

Alana added some pressure to the accelerator and sped through deep puddles that had already collected on the road. The car's wipers slashed over the windshield, smearing the rain on the glass so it was even harder for her to see. Her pulse raced out of control.

She maneuvered the car around a sharp curve. The tires squealed in protest at the excessive speed, and she checked the mirror again. The other vehicle stayed right with her, the high-beam headlights glaring into her eyes.

It certainly wasn't safe to race through a raging summer storm at ten o'clock at night, but she didn't want to face that guard on this deserted road. She had no weapon, no way to defend herself. Worse, she was exhausted and wondered if she'd be able to stand, much less fight.

Ahead of her, she finally saw the town lights. Welcome signs of civilization and help.

Going even faster, she sped toward Main Street, flanked on both sides with shops, a diner, even a white church with a steeple. Letting some vague, fuzzy memories guide her, she drove toward the center of the tiny town and spotted the sheriff's office.

Alana braked to a stop, glanced behind her and saw nothing. No car. No headlights.

No one.

Relief flooded through her. Maybe the guard had gotten scared and driven away. Still, she didn't just sit there. He might be lurking on a side street, waiting to grab her and take her back to that house in the woods.

Rain pelted her when she got out of the car. She was already cold and shivering, and the wetness didn't help. Alana ran toward the glass-front door of the sheriff's office. Each step was an effort. Her muscles were stiff, her hands throbbed from where she'd gripped the steering wheel and the dizziness was worse than it had been during her escape.

Why did everything seem out of focus? And wrong. Something was wrong. But what?

She threw open the door, and the burst of air from the AC spilled over her. It was dark in the front section of the building, but there was a light on in a room at the middle of a short narrow hall.

"Sheriff Whitley?" Her voice was barely a whisper.

She saw something move in the shadows, and a moment later, a man stepped out. Alana got just a glimpse of him before another stab of lightning flashed in the sky and the lights went out.

Oh, mercy. Had the guard done this? Was he coming after her?

"Calm down," the man said. It was Jack Whitley's voice. "If you keep breathing like that, you'll hyperventilate and I'm fresh out of paper bags." She heard his footsteps come closer. "You afraid of the dark?"

"No." Her voice still had little sound.

"Well, not to worry," Jack said as if he didn't believe her. "The storm must have knocked out the town's transformer, but we have a generator. It'll kick on in a minute or two."

He came closer still, and she caught his scent. He smelled like coffee and chocolate cake. "Did your car break down?"

Alana's teeth started to chatter. And she glanced back at the door to make sure the guard wasn't there. "Someone was following me."

Even though she couldn't see his reaction, she could feel it. He tensed and hurried past her to go to the door. "I don't see anyone," he said, looking out. "Is that your car parked out front?"

"No."

She was about to explain, but something else about him changed. The silence was heavy, making it easier to hear him draw his gun.

"I'm pretty sure the license plate matches a vehicle that was reported stolen just about an hour ago," he informed her. "The owner said the person who stole it—a woman—should be considered armed and dangerous. I'm guessing you're that woman, huh?"

Her heart jolted. Dizziness came again, and she had to lean against the wall to keep from falling.

This was certainly a complication Alana hadn't expected. That guard had some nerve to report his car stolen after he'd held her captive. And better yet—to call her armed and dangerous. The guard had been the one with the gun.

"I did steal the car," she admitted. "But I had to. They were holding me captive."

"They?" It was his cop's voice. Laced with skepticism and authority.

"A guard and a nurse. I don't know their names, but I can describe them." Well, she could if she didn't pass out first. "They held me at a house in the woods for…a long time. But I escaped."

"How'd you manage to do that?" He didn't believe that, either. She could tell from his tone.

"I spit out some of the meds they always gave me at night. And I pretended to fall asleep. Then I sneaked out of my bedroom, grabbed the guard's keys and ran. I drove away before he could stop me. But there must have been another car somewhere on the grounds, and he used it to come after me."

Jack Whitley made a sound that could have meant anything. "I need you to turn around and place your hands flat against the wall."

"You're arresting me?" She clamped her teeth over her bottom lip to keep it from shaking. Too bad she couldn't do something to stop the rest of her body from trembling. Mercy, she was freezing.

"I'm placing you in custody," he corrected, "until I

can get this straightened out. Go ahead. Hands on the wall. I need to search you."

Alana had no idea what else to do, so she complied. The painted concrete block wall was smooth against her palms, and she rested her head against it, as well, hoping it'd help her think straight.

The overhead fluorescent lights crackled on, and she heard him walk closer. "Legs slightly apart," he ordered. "And don't make any sudden moves."

Alana held her breath while he ran his left hand over her wet cotton nightgown. Down her bare legs, all the way to her equally bare feet. He repeated the process on the inside of her legs and thighs. She made a slight involuntary hitching sound when the back of his hand brushed her *there*. It was a reminder for her that she wasn't wearing any panties.

The sheriff made a similar sound, but his was more of surprise. Maybe now he'd believe that she had truly escaped with literally just the gown on her back.

"I think you've got a fever," he let her know. "You might be sick."

A fever. That might explain why she felt so horrible.

"Turn around, slowly," he said, his voice a little gentler now. "We'll go into my office, and you can sit down. If you're not feeling better after a few minutes, I can drive you to the hospital and have your temperature checked."

Alana did turn, but she kept her weight against the wall in case her legs gave way. She got her first good look at the man she had thought she could trust. Now she wasn't so sure.

It was Jack Whitley all right.

She recognized that midnight-black hair. Those

intense gunmetal-blue eyes. He wore jeans and a white shirt with his badge clipped onto a wide leather belt with a rodeo buckle. Definitely a cowboy cop in both appearance and attitude.

"I told you the truth about being held hostage," Alana insisted.

But if he heard her, there was no indication of it. His eyes widened, then narrowed. "Alana Davis?" he snarled.

"You remember me." The intense look in his eyes was scaring her.

"Yeah. I remember you."

Too bad she couldn't recall exactly what she'd done to rile him. And there was no mistaking that she'd done just that. "You helped me."

He glared at her. "Eight months ago, I pulled you from your car when you went over the bridge at Mill's Creek."

Yes. Images flashed through her mind. Icy water. She couldn't breathe. Trapped in her car. She tried to make the pieces fit and finally nodded. "You saved my life."

He didn't take his eyes off her. "And you ran away from the hospital the first chance you got. You didn't tell anyone why you were leaving or where you were going."

Alana didn't remember that at all. Why would she have done that?

"Look, I don't know what game you're playing, or why you showed up here like this. But it doesn't matter," he stated. "You're not getting Joey back."

"Joey?" She shook her head.

That riled him even more. "Are you saying you don't remember him?"

Alana forced herself to concentrate on that name. *Joey.* But it meant nothing to her.

"I'm confused about some things. Not about being held captive," she admitted. "Or you rescuing me from my car eight months ago. I know those things happened. But I think this fever's making it hard for me to concentrate."

"Right." That was all he said for several long moments. "I'll call the doctor and see if he's still at the hospital," he grumbled.

Jack shoved his gun back into his shoulder holster, caught her arm and led her to his office. He put her in the chair adjacent to his cluttered desk, and snatched up the phone.

While Jack made a call to the doctor, Alana tried to force herself to think, to assemble the memories that were fragmented in her head.

Had she really left the hospital after Jack saved her?

"My brother," she mumbled. Then she groaned. Maybe her brother, Sean, had heard about her accident and had done what he usually did.

Taken over her life.

If she'd been incapacitated, he would have had her removed from the hospital. And yes, he would have done that without telling anyone, including the sheriff. Sean wouldn't have approved of the medical care, or lack thereof, that she might be getting in a small country hospital.

And had Sean then taken her to the house in the woods?

Probably not.

Alana leaned forward so she could lay her head on Jack's desk. There weren't many bare spots on the scarred oak, but there was plenty of stuff. A flyer showed a picture of a woman with the word *missing* beneath her name, Kinley Ford. Several old newspapers. An outdated chunky computer monitor, stacks of files, not one but two chipped coffee mugs, a half-eaten slice of chocolate cake on a saucer.

She saw the fax about the car she'd supposedly stolen and would have gotten angry all over again if she hadn't spotted a framed photograph of Jack holding a baby boy. The baby wore denim overalls, a miniature cowboy hat and red boots. Both Jack and the baby were grinning.

Staring at the baby, Alana reached for the picture, but Jack snatched it away from her and put it into his center desk drawer.

"The doctor's on his way here," he relayed the second he hung up the phone.

That was good. But it wasn't the doctor or her fever that had her attention now. It was the little boy in the picture. "Who's Joey?" she asked.

Jack Whitley cursed under his breath. "What the hell's the matter with you?"

She flinched at his hard tone. "The fever, I guess. But you already know that. Please tell me—who's Joey?"

For several long moments, he didn't say anything. Alana was afraid he might not tell her. For reasons she didn't understand, it was suddenly critical that she know.

"Joey's the baby you gave birth to eight months ago," Jack informed her.

"W-what?"

Jack leaned in and got right in her face. "Joey's the

little boy you abandoned at Willow Ridge Hospital." He stabbed his index fingers at her. "And if you think you can get him back after all this time, then think again. Because Joey is *mine*."

Chapter Two

Jack felt as if someone had dropped a mountain on him.

The same woman who'd already given him the surprise of his life eight months ago on Christmas morning.

Alana Davis.

Now here she'd turned up again like a bad penny. Driving a stolen car and rattling off a story about being held captive.

A story he wasn't buying.

Alana had some explaining to do.

She didn't look much different now than she had when he'd fished her out of that frozen creek. She'd been wet then. Shivering, and scared, too.

Of course, she'd had a darn good reason to be scared. She'd nearly drowned and then had gone into shock and labor at the same time. It'd been a miracle that Jack hadn't had to deliver the newborn right there in the cab of his truck. Thankfully, he'd gotten her to the hospital and Dr. Bartolo in the nick of time.

"I had a baby?" Alana asked.

It was a question that confused and riled Jack. Of course, just about everything Alana had ever done had confused and riled him. Maybe it was the fever causing her to act this way. Maybe not. But it didn't matter. She'd made her decision about Joey the minute she walked out on him when he was barely a day old.

Now she'd have to live with that decision.

She couldn't have a lick of a claim to Joey. Jack had been the only father the little boy had ever known. He wouldn't lose him now, especially not to the mother who'd abandoned him, and Jack was certain he'd be able to convince a judge of that. She might have some legal rights as the birth mother, but those rights could be taken away.

"You don't remember giving birth to a baby," he said. Jack made sure it sounded as if he was accusing her of a Texas-size lie.

Tears sprang to her china-blue eyes, and her bottom lip trembled. She awkwardly swiped at her wet shoulder-length brown hair to push it away from her face. "Why are you saying this? Why are you telling these lies?" The tears and the trembling increased. "If I'd had a baby, I would have remembered."

But the stark fear on her pale face said differently.

"Oh, you had a baby all right. Six pounds, two ounces," he supplied.

She only shook her head.

And Jack saw something in those blue eyes that he hadn't wanted to see. Something familiar that he'd garnered from eight years of being the sheriff of Willow Ridge. The harsh reaction of a woman who just might be telling the truth.

Oh, hell.

Groaning, he sank down in his chair and stared at her.

"While we're waiting for the doctor, maybe we should start from the beginning," he suggested. Somehow, he had to make sense of all of this and arrest her for auto theft or send her on her way. "You said you remember your car going into the creek?"

Alana nodded. "I remember that. You pulled me onto the muddy bank and gave me mouth-to-mouth resuscitation. You saved my life."

So far, so good. "And then you went into labor."

Silence. For a long time. He could see the worry lines bunch up her forehead. "I don't remember that part." It seemed to break her heart to say it.

It damn near broke Jack's, too. Of course, he had more at stake than she did. Joey was his son in every way that mattered. And he wouldn't ever turn his back on that little boy the way Alana had.

"I took you to the hospital that day," Jack continued, wondering what he was going to do if he actually jogged her memory. "We got there, and you had the baby on the way into the examining room."

He watched those blue eyes to see if there was any recollection of that. But there didn't seem to be any. Only more tears. Disgusted with the sympathy those tears were producing in him, he grabbed a handful of tissues from his desk drawer and shoved them at her.

"Wipe your eyes," he insisted.

She did. It didn't help, though. More tears followed. So did a helpless-sounding throaty moan. "Why don't I remember? Why?"

"To hell if I know. You didn't seem to have a memory problem when you were there at the hospital." But even then, he'd thought there was something fishy about her story of how she'd gotten into the creek. Or what she was doing in Willow Ridge in the first place.

Alana stared at him. Blinked. "Maybe I had amnesia from the accident."

Now it was Jack's turn to shake his head. "The doctor thoroughly examined you. No head trauma. No trauma of any kind except for a bruise on your shoulder from the seat belt. I never heard of a seat belt bruise causing amnesia."

"Emotional stress, then." She sounded desperate to come up with an explanation, any explanation, of why she'd done something so despicable.

"You were fine after the delivery." Jack didn't bother to answer nicely. Every moment with her was like another mountain falling on him. "You even filled out the hospital paperwork."

Including the birth certificate.

"You nursed Joey," he continued. "Ate Christmas dinner that my aunt Tessie brought in for you. You slept a few hours. And then a little after one in the morning, you sneaked out of the hospital."

She repeated that last sentence under her breath. A moment later, a spark flared across those blue irises. "That must have been when the guard and the nurse kidnapped me."

Jack didn't bother to suppress a groan. So they were back to that story. Of course, he couldn't completely dismiss it. After all, she was sitting in his office wearing just a nightgown. A wet one at that.

The flimsy cotton clung to her breasts. It was so clingy that he could see her nipples.

He got up, grabbed a raincoat from his closet and put it over her so that it covered the entire front of her body.

For reasons he didn't understand or care to explore, seeing her breasts reminded him that she was a woman. An attractive one at that.

Jack didn't want to think about that.

He only wanted to remember that this was the person who could destroy him. All because of DNA. As far as Jack was concerned, she was just an egg donor, nothing more.

"Willow Ridge might be a hayseed town to a city girl like you, but we still have a few amenities," he explained. "Like a security camera in the hospital parking lot, for instance. That camera photographed you leaving the hospital *alone*. No guard. No nurse. Definitely no indication of a kidnapping. You left of your own free will and without anyone's coercion or assistance."

And he should know. He'd studied the tape hundreds of times trying to figure out what the devil had happened.

"You mean I left alone in the dead of winter?" she clarified. There was strong skepticism in her frail voice, and she waited until he confirmed that with a frosty nod. "Did I get into a car?"

Now, here was the confusing part. "No. You just walked away."

Jack still had that image of her in his mind, too. Wearing the bleached-out green hospital gown, cotton robe and flip-flops, she'd walked out of the front of the one-story hospital, and stumbled on the sidewalk. The cold wind had whipped at her nightclothes and her hair. She'd looked unsteady.

She'd staggered several more times as she made her way through the parking lot.

There'd only been one clear shot of her face that night.

Jack would never forget it.

It was the same frightened, tearstained, shell-shocked face that was staring back at him now.

"You said the baby's name is Joey?" she asked.

All of his muscles went stiff. He didn't want to discuss Joey with her. But he also knew he didn't have a choice. Eventually, he had to give her enough details to satisfy her curiosity so he could get her out of there.

"You named him," he reminded her.

Another blink. "Did I?"

He couldn't contain his smirk, but beneath it, his concerns were snowballing. "You did. You said you named him after your kid brother who died when you were a child." And he braced himself.

Alana hugged his raincoat closer to her. "I remember my little brother, Joey. And I remember I was wearing a green hospital gown and robe when I woke up at the house in the woods."

Jack actually welcomed the change in subject, even though he knew it could only be temporary.

Eventually she'd ask more about Joey.

"What else do you remember about the house, the guard and the nurse?" he asked.

She hesitated a moment. "Everything, I think. It was December twenty-sixth when I woke up in that house. So I must have been there all this time." Alana's eyes met his. "Why did they hold me captive?"

Jack shrugged. "You're the only one who'll be able to answer that."

Their eyes stayed connected until she lurched at the sound of the front door opening. Because he was on edge, Jack automatically reached for his gun and went to the door. But the gun wasn't necessary. The tall, lanky visitor was Dr. Keith Bartolo.

"Doc's here," Jack relayed to Alana, only because she looked ready to jump out of her skin.

"Jack," the doctor grumbled. He pulled off his rain-beaded felt hat, and with his leather medical bag gripped in his right hand, he made his way down the hall.

Jack had known the doctor most of his life, since the man had moved to Willow Ridge over twenty-three years ago and set up a practice. Jack also knew when Bartolo wasn't in a good mood. Apparently, the fiftysomething-year-old doc didn't like being called out after hours during a storm. Jack knew how the man felt. He rarely worked late these days because of Joey, but here he was at ten thirty going a second round with Alana Davis when he was supposed to be finishing up paperwork so he could take the weekend off.

"You said you had a sick prisoner," Dr. Bartolo prompted. He headed in the direction of the lone jail cell at the far end of the hall.

"She's in my office," Jack corrected.

The doctor lifted a caramel-brown eyebrow, and Jack stepped to the side so the man could enter. The doc and Alana looked at each other, and Jack didn't know which one of them was more surprised.

Alana swallowed hard. "I know you."

"Of course you do." Dr. Bartolo stared at her. "I was the attending physician when Jack brought you to the hospital last Christmas."

That was it. Apparently that was all the bedside manner he intended to dispense. The doctor plopped his bag onto Jack's desk, unzipped it and pulled out a digital thermometer. After putting a plastic sleeve over the tip, he stuck it in Alana's mouth.

"Why is she a prisoner?" the doctor asked as the thermometer beeped once.

"She stole a car."

Even though Alana didn't say anything out loud, her eyes said plenty. Jack could almost hear her giving him a tongue-lashing. Yes, she'd stolen the car. She'd admitted that. But according to her, it'd been to escape.

So, was it true?

He could check with the sheriff who'd posted the stolen car report and get the name of the person who had filed the claim. That would lead him to Alana's so-called guard. Jack hoped this wasn't some kind of lovers' quarrel. But he immediately rethought that. Maybe that would be the best solution for him. Find whoever was behind this so she could drop the amnesia act.

If it *was* an act.

The thermometer made a series of rapid beeps. Dr. Bartolo pulled it from her mouth and looked at the tiny screen. "Your temp's just a little over a hundred. Not too high. Any idea what's wrong with you?"

She shook her head.

"Okay." Dr. Bartolo didn't appear to be any more convinced of that than Jack did of her amnesia story. He flicked the plastic disposable tip into the trash and placed the thermometer back into his bag. "Are you taking any meds?"

Alana glanced at Jack. "No."

Jack frowned. "She said a guard and a nurse gave her

some sedatives, and they'd been doing that for some time now," he explained. And he didn't think she'd forgotten that already. Her eyes narrowed slightly as if she hadn't wanted to share that information with the doctor.

"Sedatives?" the doctor questioned. "What kind?"

She shook her head again, causing Jack to huff. Before the doctor's arrival, she'd been chatty, so why hush now? "The kind of sedatives that might cause memory loss," Jack provided. "Or not. She could be making that part up."

That caused some concern in the doctor's eyes. "If there's a possibility of memory loss, she needs to be hospitalized. I'd also need to do a tox screen to see if there's anything in her blood."

"Would a fever that low cause her to hallucinate?" Jack asked Dr. Bartolo. "Or could sedatives do that?"

He lifted his shoulder. "Not the fever but possibly the sedatives. Why? What makes you think she's hallucinating?"

"A couple of things, but we can try to figure out all of that at the hospital." And once he had more details, he'd have to deal with the stolen car issue. It was entirely possible that the sheriff of the town where the stolen car complaint was filed would come and take Alana back to face those charges.

Jack hated that he felt relief about that.

But he did. The sooner he got Alana Davis out of Joey's life, the better.

"I have to go to the bathroom," Alana announced, standing. But she had to catch his desk to stop herself from falling. Or maybe it was all an act to get him to feel sorry for her.

"Across the hall." Jack pointed in that direction. Both Jack and the doctor watched her as she made her way into the tiny room.

"Okay," Dr. Bartolo said the moment the bathroom door closed. "What's this all about? Did she come back to town to try to get Joey from you?"

"I don't know." There was so much about this that didn't make sense. "She says she doesn't remember giving birth to him."

"Is that so?" Bartolo stayed quiet a moment. "I guess that means she can't or won't say why she left town the way she did."

"She says she doesn't remember that, either. But she does remember being taken captive after leaving the hospital." Jack paused to figure out how best to phrase this. "Is it possible she's crazy?"

"It's possible," the doctor readily agreed. "After all, most normal women wouldn't just abandon their newborn the way she did."

True. Her behavior here tonight hadn't convinced him that she was doing any better than she had been eight months ago.

"But maybe it's something equally obvious," the doctor continued. "Maybe she's broken the law. Maybe she's a criminal, and she's telling you she has memory loss to cover up something else."

Jack mulled that over and cursed.

He bolted toward the bathroom. The door was locked, of course. So he pounded on it. "Alana, open up!"

Nothing.

Not so much as a sniffle.

Though he was riled enough to bash down the door, he resisted. Because he knew it wouldn't do any good. There was a small window in the bathroom, and if his instincts were right, Alana had already used it, to escape.

Jack raced down the hall, past the jail cell and headed for the rear exit. It was raining harder now, but that didn't slow him down. He ran to the east exterior side of the building, to the sliver of an alleyway that separated the sheriff's office from City Hall. The narrow space was made even narrower by a dark green Dumpster stuck right in the middle. And it was pitch black.

Someone screamed.

Alana.

With his heart pounding now, he drew his gun and raced around the Dumpster. Jack spotted her white nightgown. She appeared to be struggling with someone.

"What's going on?" he called out.

Just like that, the struggle stopped, and Alana fell back against the wall. Hard. She stayed on her feet and pointed in the opposition direction from where he was standing.

Jack thought he heard footsteps, but he couldn't be sure because of the pounding rain. Keeping his gun ready just in case, he went to her.

"Did you see him?" Alana asked.

"See who?" Jack automatically looked around.

"It was the guard from the house," she said, still pointing. "He was trying to make me go back."

Jack heard another sound.

A car engine.

He sprinted to the alley opening that led to Main Street, and stopped just short of the sidewalk. Using the sheriff's office for cover, he glanced around the corner.

A dark-colored car sped away.

Mud or something had been smeared over the license plate, and he couldn't even get a glimpse of the driver because of the heavily tinted windows and the darkness.

It was possible the driver was just a visitor. Some innocent guy who was in the wrong place at the wrong time. But just in case, Jack turned to get his patrol car. He simply wanted to ask the driver a few questions. But then he looked back and saw Alana, just as she collapsed on the ground.

Chapter Three

Alana heard voices. They were only whispers at first. But they became clearer within just a few seconds.

She didn't open her eyes. Not yet. She waited, listening, trying to figure out what was going on.

Was it safe?

Or did she need to be prepared to run again?

Judging from the sterile smell and the feel of the bed beneath her, she wasn't back at the house in the woods. Nor was she in the alley next to the sheriff's office. She was in a hospital. And the voice, at least one of them, belonged to Jack Whitley. He was talking to Dr. Bartolo.

She peeked out. Definitely a hospital. The walls and bedding were stark white, and there was an IV in the back of her hand. Sunlight threaded through the blind slats and onto the thermal blanket that covered her.

Neither the guard nor the nurse who'd held her captive was there. Everything felt safe. Which was a facade, of course. It wasn't safe unless Jack had caught the guard after he'd attacked her in the alley.

Maybe he had.

The last thing she remembered before losing consciousness was Jack going after him. If he'd succeeded, then perhaps the nightmare was over.

Well, part of it, anyway.

There was still the issue of her son.

Her mind no longer felt like sludge, and Alana didn't have to think hard to remember everything. She was a jewelry designer. Born and raised in San Antonio. One sibling, her older brother, Sean. She had friends and a life that had disappeared eight months ago.

The day she went into labor.

She could recall each pain. Every moment. Including the birth of her precious son. She'd loved him instantly. A kind of love she hadn't thought was possible until she'd held him in her arms for the first time.

But there were blanks. The missing twenty-four hours of her life that followed the delivery. And even some of the time immediately before it. They were crucial gaps of time—she had no idea what had put her in that creek or what had happened to make her leave her newborn son and walk out into the cold December night. She only knew the end result. She'd been held captive, escaped and then nearly been killed again.

"You're awake," she heard Jack say. He walked closer, crammed his hands into the pockets of his jeans and stood over her.

He was still wearing the same clothes he'd had on the night before. And he hadn't shaved. A dark, desperado stubble covered his chin, and there were smudgy circles under his eyes. He probably hadn't slept.

"Why am I in the hospital?" she asked.

"The fever for one thing. It's gone now, but Dr. Bartolo thinks you had a virus of some kind. You also hit your head when you fell in the alley. He needed to check and make sure it wasn't serious. It's just a bad bump." He glanced at Dr. Bartolo on the other side of the room before his attention returned to her. "Don't you remember?"

She didn't have to think hard for those memories to flood through her. Plus, the left side of her head was throbbing. "Yes. I remember. I was trying to get away because I was scared of the doctor. *And you.* But you caught me. Did you catch the man, too?"

Jack shook his head. "Sorry."

Fear instantly returned. If the man had gotten to her once, he could get to her again. But Alana didn't think that was her biggest concern right now. There was something guarded about Jack's expression. For one thing, he wasn't glaring at her. In fact, he was treating her like a patient.

"Did you see the person who tried to grab me in the alley?" she wanted to know.

"Not really."

"It was the guard," Alana concluded, though she hadn't actually seen his face. "You'll have to find him."

Jack nodded, but it seemed to be a gesture to appease her. He eased his hands from his pockets, dragged a chair closer and sat down beside her bed.

Oh, no. She got a really bad feeling about this. He was obviously about to have a heart-to-heart chat with her.

"After I got you to the hospital last night, I called your brother, Sean, in San Antonio," Jack explained. "Do you remember him?"

"Of course," she said after she got her teeth unclenched. Great. Just great. Now her overly protective big brother knew everything she'd told Jack. But that also meant that Sean had known she'd been held captive.

He was probably already on his way to Willow Ridge.

Sean would powerhouse his way into the hospital and try to take over. His goal would be to get her away from there so he could convince her that she didn't want to try to claim her son.

"I remember almost everything," Alana mumbled. Including her brother's objection to her being pregnant. Sean had hated the fact that she planned to become a single mom. Not because he was truly concerned about the challenges that might bring, but because of appearances. He believed their conservative business associates would think less of Alana and therefore think less of their company and him. Plus, Sean had also expressed concern that Alana's focus might be on a child and not solely on her career.

"Good." Jack followed that with a crisp nod. "I'm glad you're getting your memory back."

She'd been ready to try to get out of the bed, but that stopped her. "Good?" Alana contested. "Okay, what's wrong?"

He scrubbed his hand over his face. "You recall why you walked out of here eight months ago?"

Alana hated to admit this, but she had no choice. If she told Jack as much as she knew, he might be able to help her put the pieces together. "No. But I know I gave birth to Joey. And I know I love him. I also want to see him. Now."

Jack stayed quiet a moment. "That wouldn't be a

good idea. You have a virus, remember, and in case it's something more, it'll be another ten hours or so before the antibiotics take full effect. You wouldn't want to make him sick, would you?" His tone was sympathetic enough, but there was a lot of emotion and anger simmering right beneath the surface.

"Oh, I get it," Alana grumbled. "My brother told you to be nice to me."

"Among other things," Jack admitted. "He's coming to take you home."

Alana wanted to curse. "How much time do I have before Sean gets here?"

"An hour. Maybe two. He said he'd be here around noon, and it's a little after ten right now."

She sat up. "I don't want him to see me like this. And I don't want to go with him."

Jack caught her arm and eased her back down onto the bed. "Sean told me that Joey's birth father was dead."

That clenched her teeth again. "You obviously had a long conversation."

"We did. But Sean and I had that particular discussion eight months ago when I was trying to track you down."

Everything inside her went still. She hadn't thought of it sooner, but of course Jack would have tried to find her. Too bad he hadn't. It would have saved her eight months of captivity, and that was just the beginning. It had also cost her time with her precious baby. She'd missed so much already.

Too much.

She wouldn't miss any more.

"Sean didn't know why you ran off the way you did," Jack continued. "But he had a theory. He thought it was because you were clinically depressed."

Maybe. But that didn't feel right, either. "Depressed, why?"

"Because of the death of Joey's birth father, Neil Franklin."

She shook her head. "My relationship with Neil had been over for months before he died. In fact, I ended things with him when I learned I was pregnant and he said he didn't want to be a father."

There were no gaps in those particular memories, including the big blowup when Neil had even questioned if he was indeed the father of her unborn child. That accusation had been more than enough to cause Alana to walk out. But then she'd had to listen to months of her brother saying "I told you so" and trying to pressure her to give the child up for adoption.

And then all those memories collided with her present situation.

"Why all these questions about Sean and Neil? Did Sean do something to get me to abandon Joey here at the hospital? Is that why I left?" she demanded.

Jack didn't jump to deny it. Nor did he confirm it, either. He took his time answering, and the moment he opened his mouth, his phone rang. He jerked it from his pocket as if he'd been expecting an important call.

"I have to take this," he said, and he got up, stepped outside and shut the door.

Alana wanted to listen to his conversation—it might pertain to her. But Dr. Bartolo put her chart aside and walked closer. "I got your lab results back. You had traces of a drug called Rohypnol in your system."

"Rohypnol," she repeated. "The date rape drug?"

The doctor nodded and must have noticed that she was on the verge of panicking. "You weren't sexually assaulted," he continued. He reached over and began to remove the IV. "But there was enough of the drug in your system to explain your memory loss."

God knows how many doses of the Rohypnol she'd been given. The nurse and guard had forced her to take it almost daily. She was certain of that. What Alana wasn't certain about was discussing it with the doctor. For some reason, she didn't trust him. Had he done something to make her feel this way? Or was she just being paranoid?

If so, she had a reason for the paranoia. Someone had also tried to take her from that alley. He'd grabbed her, hard, and was dragging her away when Jack arrived.

"I delivered your son," the doctor added a moment later.

"Yes." She studied his body language. His forehead was bunched. His breathing, short and a little rough. "I don't suppose you know why I left the hospital?"

She expected a quick denial. But it didn't come. His breathing got even shorter. "You said some things when you were in labor. Maybe it means nothing. But you said someone had run you off the road."

Alana forced her mind to the crash. The images were all there. Cold and crisp. Images of her in her car in the water. But nothing of what'd happened moments before impact.

"I told Jack what you said, and he checked out the

creek road again," the doctor explained. "He didn't find any tread marks or any other sign to indicate that you had slammed on the brakes or swerved to miss going into the creek."

"That proves nothing. Someone could still have been after me," she quickly pointed out. She winced a little when he pulled the IV needle from her hand.

"You're right." He dabbed the IV puncture with some cotton and then slipped a bandage over it. "Something sure had you spooked. You remember what that was?"

This suddenly felt like an interrogation. Or a threat to remind her that remembering wouldn't be a good idea.

Alana shook her head. "I don't know. Do you?"

His head jerked back a little in a gesture of surprise. "Of course not. I told Jack everything that went on and everything you said to me."

She wasn't so sure. "What else did I say?"

"Some of it was rambling," he readily answered. But he didn't say anything for several moments. "I got the feeling you were withholding information, that you were in some kind of trouble. Were you?"

Probably. But she kept that to herself.

Alana went back through those memory gaps. If someone had indeed run her off the road, then something had happened to precipitate it. Maybe it was as simple as a case of road rage. Some hotheaded driver had cut her off and caused the accident.

Yes, that was possible. Better than the alternative. But why hadn't there been any sign of her slamming on the brakes? And what had she been doing in Willow Ridge?

"When you were in labor, you mentioned an important meeting," the doctor continued. He took her chart and jotted down something on it. He didn't look at her. He kept his focus on whatever he was writing. "Guess you don't remember that, either?"

She didn't, and even though Alana tried hard to recall any details about that, she drew a blank.

"An important meeting," Dr. Bartolo repeated. "Maybe it had something to do with your job?"

This chat was making her more uncomfortable by the minute. She looked around in case she needed an escape route. But that wasn't necessary. Jack came back through the door.

Alana cursed the relief she felt at seeing him. For some reason, she trusted him. However, he didn't extend much trust to her. He shoved his phone back into his pocket and stared at her. He didn't sit or offer her any more pseudo sympathy.

"You're looking at me as if I'm crazy," she said.

"Sorry." But he kept staring at her. "Do the names Ted Moore and Margaret Vargas ring any bells?"

"No. Should they?"

"Yeah." He paused. A long time. "They should."

Mercy. Was this another blank spot in her memory? If so, it must be a critical one. "Do they have something to do with Joey?"

"Not really." Jack nodded at the doctor, a gesture the two of them must have understood, because the doctor excused himself and left the room.

This conversation must be about to turn ugly.

And then it hit her. A horrible thought. "Did the man in the alley go after Joey?"

"No. Joey's fine."

But she didn't believe him. "I have to see him. I have to make sure he's okay. And don't remind me about this virus. I don't have to get close to him to make sure he's safe."

He clamped his hand on her arm when she tried to get up. "You aren't going to see him, Alana."

Alana pushed his hand away. "You have no legal right to keep my son from me."

"Wanna bet?"

She froze. Because that didn't sound like an idle threat. "What does that mean?"

"It means when you filled out the birth certificate, you listed me as the father."

Had she? Yes. She had. Why, though, she didn't know. "But you're not his father and a DNA test will prove that."

"Biologically, Joey's not my son, but he is legally. When we couldn't find you, I petitioned the courts for custody, and since your brother, Sean, was Joey's next of kin, he agreed. He gave me sole guardianship."

She clenched her hands tightly. Alana didn't doubt that Sean had done this. He'd never wanted her to have the baby. "Well, I can change that. I can petition the courts, too—"

"No judge will give you custody, Alana."

Again, it wasn't an empty threat. He had something to back it up. "Why not?"

"Because you weren't held captive. The guard and the nurse I mentioned. Ted Moore and Margaret Vargas. They've contacted law enforcement agencies to report your disappearance."

Alana shook her head. She didn't understand. "My disappearance?"

"More like your escape," Jack clarified. "Alana, you were declared insane. For the past eight months you've been confined to a private mental institution."

Chapter Four

Alana didn't have much color in her cheeks, but Jack's announcement drained what little she did have. She swallowed hard and eased her head back onto the pillow. Her eyelids fluttered down.

She looked beaten and overwhelmed.

Jack knew exactly how she felt.

For eight months, he'd dreaded Alana's return, but with each passing day, it'd been easier and easier for him to convince himself that she wouldn't come back. That she wouldn't fall back into his life and try to claim Joey.

Yet here she was. A force to be reckoned with. A woman to fear. He should be bracing himself to do battle. But unfortunately, like her he was feeling overwhelmed himself. And empathy was starting to creep into this equation. But that wasn't the only problem.

There was this physical pull he had for her.

He was sure those two emotions were connected. That, and the fact that Alana was attractive. It would have been hard not to notice that about her. But empathy and attraction could cause him to lose focus. That, in turn, could cause him to lose Joey.

"So now I'm crazy," she mumbled. Alana chuckled, but there was no humor in it. She opened her eyes and blinked back tears. "I'm not crazy, Jack. I'm not."

He didn't want to offer an opinion on that. Instead, it was best to go ahead and put everything out in the open. "There was a court order committing you to the institution."

Her gaze slashed to his, and she swiped the tears from her face. "I want to see it."

He nodded. "It's being faxed." He wanted to see it, as well.

"And I want to speak to Ted Moore and Margaret Vargas. I want them to explain why they gave me a date rape drug. That's hardly the medication a reputable institution would dispense to a so-called patient."

Jack knew about the drug. Dr. Bartolo had already told him. He wanted to ask that same question himself. In fact, he wanted to ask Ted and Margaret a lot of questions.

Because something wasn't adding up.

More than anything, he needed Alana's situation to make sense. If she was legally insane, then he could send her back to an institution. She wouldn't be able to take Joey. He didn't relish the thought of Alana being crazy, but he was desperate to hang on to his son.

But as a lawman, he also needed the truth.

He cursed himself. This need for justice had been an obsession most of his life, and it'd had devastating consequences. His own father was in prison because of it, and while most would say that the man deserved to be behind bars, Jack would always remember that it was his testimony that had turned the key to his father's prison cell.

"Margaret was the one who had the authorities put out an APB on you," Jack explained. "She's also the one who'll be faxing the court order."

She stared up at the ceiling, and her mouth tightened. "Let me guess. My brother initiated that court order? He's the one who had me sent to that place."

"I'm not sure." But it was a darn good guess. When Jack had met Sean eight months earlier, the man had made it crystal clear that he didn't want Alana raising Joey. Sean thought she was not "emotionally equipped" to be a single parent. Still, it seemed extreme that Sean would have his sister committed. Unless he truly thought she was insane. Then, Sean might have wanted to hide her away so she wouldn't be a liability to their business and so she could discretely get some help.

"Margaret didn't know where Ted was," Jack added. "She said she hasn't seen him since last night when he went after you."

"Well, I know where he was. He was in that alley. He tried to hurt me."

Jack didn't dispute that. But he was sure, though, that his body language was suggesting some doubt. "See, that's one of the things that doesn't add up. The APB was out there. Plus, you were right next to a sheriff's office. If it'd been Ted in that alley, he would have just walked inside and asked me for assistance." He paused. "And I would have given it to him."

"So, who do you think it was in the alley?" she demanded.

A hallucination caused by the fever and the drugs already in her system. Except Jack had seen that car with the mud-smeared plates. Still, a strange car didn't mean this Ted had tried to grab her.

"If Ted had come to apprehend you, why would he have run?" Jack asked. "He had a court order to keep you confined. The law was on his side, not yours."

Another punch of frustration rushed through her eyes. "Maybe that court order isn't worth the paper it's being faxed on."

"Maybe. That's one of the things I might be able to determine when I see the document."

And when he questioned Ted and Margaret. Whenever that would be. The woman hadn't exactly volunteered to come to Willow Ridge, which meant Jack would have to make a trip to the Sauder Mental Health Facility about an hour's drive away. Margaret hadn't been chatty about the exact location, claiming that the place was private to prevent the media from finding it and the occasional famous patients who entered the facility for drug rehab.

Margaret's explanation had made him even more uneasy. But he couldn't go until he had things stabilized with Alana. Fortunately, he'd already gotten Ted and Margaret's photos from the online database of drivers' licenses, and he'd run computer checks. Neither had criminal records, but Jack had asked his deputy to do a little digging to see if anything flagged.

"When the fax arrives," Alana continued, "I want you to read that court order word for word. I'll do the same. But first, I'll have to battle my brother." She lifted her head from the pillow again, and this time she pushed his hand away when he tried to stop her. "I need some clothes. I don't want Sean to see me like this. I'm sure

I look frail and weak. It'll only give him more ammunition to try to have me recommitted."

Jack couldn't argue with that, but Alana wasn't ready to be up and moving around. Still, he didn't stop her. "I can't guarantee the doctor will let you leave the hospital, but I'll see what I can do about getting you something else to wear."

She'd gathered up the blanket to drape around her. Her gaze met his. "Thank you."

He didn't want her thanks. He didn't want empathy. He didn't want to feel that she was getting railroaded.

But he did.

Damn it. He did.

Jack stepped outside the room, and welcomed the moment he had to himself. He didn't usually have trouble being objective, especially since Alana was officially part of an investigation now. But she was also a huge threat to his happiness. That was coloring his objectivity.

When he spotted Sara Murphy, a nurse and a woman he'd known his entire life, he walked up the hall to her. "Could you possibly scrounge up some street clothes for the patient?" Jack hitched his thumb toward Alana's door.

Sara nodded and shifted a pink wad of sugary-scented gum in her mouth so she could answer him. "Sure will." She volleyed her doe-brown eyes between Jack and the door. "I heard what's going on, and I'm sorry. She's here to try to take little Joey, isn't she?"

Jack settled for saying, "It's complicated."

"Not so complicated. You love that boy. Everybody around here knows that." Sara patted his arm. "Have you learned anything more about the night she wandered out of the hospital?"

"No."

Sara glanced around as if to make sure no one was listening, and stepped closer. "Look, I'm on your side. I don't want that woman back here. But you know I've had my worries about her from the start."

Yeah. He did. He'd interviewed Sara several times. "You don't think Alana left the hospital voluntarily that night eight months ago."

"And I still don't. I saw her an hour before she disappeared, and she was fit as a fiddle. She talked about Joey, about their future together. She was talking about taking Mommy and Me classes, for heaven's sake." Sara shook her head. "And then bam! an hour later, she walks out into the freezing night without giving a second thought to leaving her baby behind."

Since it'd been a while since those interviews, Jack asked the obvious. "You're sure you didn't see anyone go into Alana's room that night?"

She flexed her eyebrows. "Just Doc Bartolo."

There it was again. That same punch of doubt that had come eight months ago. Dr. Bartolo had been the last credible person to see Alana. She'd been fine, he insisted. Since the doctor had never given Jack a reason to distrust him, he'd believed him.

Except there was a niggling doubt in the back of his mind. Jack had discovered that looking at Joey had dimmed those doubts.

"You did the right thing, taking that baby the way you did," Sara insisted.

Did I? Jack asked himself.

Thankfully, he didn't pose that question to Sara. He spotted Deputy Reyes Medina making his way down the hall toward him. At six-three and well over two hundred pounds, Reyes was impossible to miss. He had the face and the coloring of his Comanche ancestors, but his expression was all cop. He walked, looked and talked as if he were ready to kick someone's butt into the next county.

It took Jack a moment to realize Reyes wasn't alone. He saw something behind the deputy, and after Reyes moved a little to the side, Jack got another surprise he didn't want.

His aunt Tessie was there, and she was holding Joey.

Jack groaned some ripe profanity. This was not the place he wanted his son.

"I'll get those clothes for Ms. Davis," Sara mumbled, excusing herself.

Jack heard her, but he didn't respond, instead making a beeline for his aunt.

"Is it true?" Tessie asked. She'd obviously dressed in a hurry. No makeup, not that she wore much anyway. Her salt-white hair was in disarray, and her Coke-bottle-green eyes were wide with concern. "Is that woman really here in the hospital?"

Jack caught her arm to stop her from moving any closer to Alana's room. "She's here. I was going to tell you, but I haven't had a chance."

Unlike Reyes and Tessie, Joey wasn't showing much concern. He grinned from ear to ear and reached for Jack. Jack pulled his son into his arms and gave himself a moment to be a father. He could have sworn his blood pressure dropped to normal. The knot in his stomach eased up. And for a few precious seconds, all was right with the world.

"I told Tessie she shouldn't be here," Reyes grumbled.

Tessie started her defense before Reyes finished the last word of his sentence. "I wanted to see her. I want to make her understand that she can't come back after all these months and take Joey."

"It's not a good time to do that," Jack countered. He couldn't tell Tessie that Alana would try to take Joey. Jack didn't even want to say the words aloud.

There was a sound behind him, and judging from Tessie's and Reyes's reactions, Jack knew what it was. He quickly handed Joey to Tessie. "Take him home please."

She nodded but kept her attention fastened to the other end of the hall. One glance over his shoulder confirmed that Alana was there, standing in the doorway of her room. She had the blanket draped around her like a robe and was looking at Joey. She started toward him.

"The virus," Jack reminded her. "You'll make him sick."

Alana froze. Thank God. If it hadn't been for her illness, Alana would have tried to wrench Joey from Tessie's arms. Joey would have been confused. Frightened. And the contact would no doubt have given Alana even more determination to take the child she'd given birth to.

Tessie turned and hurried back toward the exit. Jack went to Alana, to make sure she stayed put. When he reached her, he saw her tears, even though she was doing her level best to blink them away.

"He's so beautiful," she whispered, her attention still

focused over his shoulder where Tessie had been standing just seconds earlier.

"Yes, he is."

"Joey has my hair color." She touched her fingers to her own saddle-brown locks. "What about his eyes? What color are they?"

"Blue." Like Alana's. Jack didn't volunteer that, though. His heart already felt as if it were being crushed.

"Blue," she repeated with a determined nod. "I'm seeing him tomorrow." It wasn't a request. "The medicine will have kicked in. I won't be contagious. I'll see my baby."

Jack was already trying to figure out a way to stop that. Or a way for him to deal with what might be inevitable. Because even if Alana was sent back to that institution, it didn't mean she was out of the picture when it came to Joey. She'd hire a lawyer. She'd fight. And now that she knew she had a son, she wouldn't back down. But as the only father Joey had ever known, he wouldn't back down, either.

Reyes handed Jack some papers. The first was a fax with the photo of a woman. The FBI had already sent him her picture, and it was on his desk. "Kinley Ford?" Jack read aloud.

"She's the missing woman the Rangers and FBI are looking for. It's possible she's in the area."

Well, it wouldn't be the first time. Nine months ago Kinley Ford had been in town, and even though she hadn't been responsible, three people had been killed. It'd been one of the few murder cases Jack had ever had to handle, and he didn't want to have to deal with her now. "Does she have anything to do with Alana?"

"Not that I can tell, but a lot of people are anxious to find her. The FBI wants us to put flyers with her picture around town."

Jack intended to do that, but it would have to wait. He looked at the other papers Reyes had given him. Alana's commitment papers. With them were two black-and-white pictures. When Jack glanced at them, he remembered that Joey wasn't the only issue here.

"I got her commitment papers a little over an hour ago and made some calls," Reyes explained. "I'm trying to track down the judge who signed them."

Good. That was a start.

"I also showed those around." Reyes pointed to the photos of Ted Moore and Margaret Vargas. The deputy glanced at Alana.

"And?" Jack prompted, giving Reyes permission to go on.

"They just arrived in town. So did her brother, Sean. All three are in the hospital lobby."

"Here?" Jack and Alana said in unison. Apparently Margaret had decided to come to town after all.

Alana's tone was laced with anger. She seemed to welcome this unexpected visit. Jack did, too, in a way. But he wanted this meeting to happen at the sheriff's office since it would likely turn into an interrogation. Maybe even an arrest.

Reyes nodded. "Margaret said she left the institution as soon as she faxed the commitment papers to us. Said she figured it was best that she speak to Alana and you in person."

Jack wasn't so sure of that.

"I told them to wait in the lobby until I cleared everything with you," Reyes explained. "According to the pair, they didn't arrive with the brother. It's a coincidence that they're all here together at exactly the same time."

Jack wasn't a strong believer in coincidences. It could be that Sean had a reason to want to dissociate himself from the pair. Especially from Ted—the man might have crossed a legal line or two if he truly had gone after Alana the way she said he had.

"Before you see to them, I think you should know what I learned," the deputy went on. "When I showed those pictures around town this morning, the new waitress that Bella hired over at the diner said she saw that man, Ted, late last night."

"Where?" Jack asked, though he already suspected the answer.

"In front of your office. She said the guy came running out of the alley, jumped in his car and drove away. She said he looked like he was up to no good."

"He was," Alana assured them. She turned to him. "I told you."

So she had. Jack would have liked to explain the man's behavior. But he couldn't. Unless Ted was trying to cover up the fact that a patient had escaped and he didn't want to get in trouble for a security infraction. But that didn't make sense. Once the man realized he hadn't contained Alana, then why hadn't he stayed? Why get in his car and leave without alerting someone in the sheriff's office?

Jack heard the footsteps, looked up and realized he might not have to wait long for those answers. Sean and his guests hadn't stayed put in the lobby despite the deputy's order. They were coming up the hall, and judging from their expressions, they were there to take Alana back to the institution.

Of course, that led Jack to another question.

Was he going to let them?

Chapter Five

Alana knew she should be bracing herself for the meeting with her brother and the two people who'd held her captive. She should also be preparing for a fight in case Margaret and Ted attempted to apprehend her.

But she had trouble focusing.

The fever and drugs weren't to blame this time. Her thoughts were scattered. Only moments earlier she'd seen her son.

"Joey," she said under her breath.

Just that glimpse of him had been enough for her to know this child was hers. Love was instant. Strong. And she would use that love to give her strength. She would get her son back. But first, she had to deal with the three obstacles coming her way.

Four, she corrected.

Because Jack might turn out to be the biggest obstacle of all.

"Alana," her brother greeted, but there was no warmth in it. Not that she expected it from him. Sean was her only living brother, but over the years, they'd become more business partners than siblings. And because he was older, he had declared himself her boss and keeper.

"Why don't we take this into the room?" Jack suggested. He looked back at his deputy. "Stay close just in case."

Alana wasn't leaving with her brother, Margaret or Ted, and she would use physical force if necessary to stop them from taking her.

With the hulking deputy choosing to wait outside the door, they filed into her hospital room, each casting glances at her. She threw some glances right back at them.

"Where do I start?" she mumbled. She had a list of questions and accusations. She decided to begin with Ted because she could still feel his hands on her when he tried to grab her in the alley. "Explain what you were trying to do to me last night."

Ted's Adam's apple bobbed on his thin throat. It was the only thing thin about him. He had bulky shoulders and arms, and his shaved head made him seem even more fearsome. "I was trying to do my job and bring you back to the Sauder facility."

"So you admit you were here in Willow Ridge?" Jack asked.

"Of course. Ms. Davis is a patient, and it's my job to make sure she stays confined until the judge says differently. We were instructed that she could be a danger to herself and others."

That must have been Margaret's cue to bring out the paper she had tucked beneath her arm. Like Ted, Margaret was no lightweight. She was close to six feet tall and had an athletic build. There'd been times when Margaret had held her down and forced her to take the sedating drugs.

"And here's a notice from the judge that your confinement has *not* been terminated," Margaret announced. "I had him fax it to the hospital so I could show you." There was a victorious glimmer in her ice-gray eyes when she looked at Alana. "That means you're to be returned to Sauder immediately."

Alana wasn't unaffected by the threat. Other than Jack, and he was iffy, she didn't have an ally in the room.

Jack took the paper from Margaret and glanced over it. While he was doing that, Alana turned her attention to the biggest rat in the room, her brother.

As usual, Sean was dressed to perfection. Italian suit. A pair of those pricey leather shoes he had custom-made for him. Genetically, they looked alike with his light brown hair and blue eyes. But their personalities were as different as night and day.

Just being near him caused her blood to boil, and she had to fight to hang on to her temper. "You surrendered custody of my son to Jack. I'd like to know why."

He shrugged, showing no concern as to what he'd put her through. "Because I couldn't find you, and because I didn't want to raise the kid myself. Besides, I figured Jack would make a good father."

It was the flippant answer she'd expected. Still, it didn't make it easier to hear, or accept. "So you had me locked up in a mental institution."

"Not me. I didn't do that."

"I don't believe you."

Another shrug. He slid his hands into his pants pockets. "Believe what you will, but I had nothing to do with it. I couldn't even find you, much less have you committed."

Strange. Her brother was a coldhearted jerk, but she hadn't known him to be a liar. But if he was telling the truth, then who had put her in that place?

"You have the judge's name?" she asked Jack.

"Marvin Pierce," he read from the paper that he'd taken from Margaret. "Ring any bells?"

"None." But there were a lot of confusing things about this situation. She turned back to Margaret. "Who paid for me to stay at the facility?"

"I don't know."

Jack spoke up before Alana could. "Then, I need the name of the facility's business manager."

Margaret shook her head. "I manage it and have done for the past eight months. Ms. Davis was our only patient, though I'd been informed that in the past, there were others. Some of them were celebrities who wanted to go through rehab while they hid from the paparazzi."

Alana obviously wasn't the only one who found it odd that she was the sole patient. Even her brother lowered his chin and angled a questioning glance at both Ted and Margaret. Jack did more than glance.

"Then who paid your salaries?" he asked.

Margaret looked at Ted before she answered. "All payments came from the Sauder Foundation. I just assumed Ms. Davis's family was paying the foundation for her residential care since there wasn't any paperwork for medical insurance."

"Not me, I wasn't paying," Sean volunteered. "If my sister had needed psychological help, I would have sent her to Europe. No need to announce that sort of thing to business associates and friends by keeping her in the state."

All of them looked at Alana. "Trust me, I didn't pay to

have myself committed. I'd just given birth to a beautiful healthy baby boy. The only thing I wanted was to be with him. So I wouldn't have hired someone to lock me away."

Jack made a throaty sound of agreement. And she knew that cost him. He probably wanted nothing more than for these people to take her, but she was praying the lawman in him would want the truth. Even if the truth cost him custody of the child he'd raised.

"We have the paper to return her to the facility," Margaret reminded them. She stepped forward.

Jack blocked her path. "Alana can't leave. She's here because she's sick. She has a virus, and it's highly contagious."

Margaret dropped back a step. So did Ted. Sean stayed put, probably because he felt he was immune to such mundane things.

"I can take her home," her brother insisted. "She can receive medical treatment there."

"I don't want to go home." Alana took a deep breath to continue the fight, but it wasn't necessary.

"She's staying put," Jack interjected. "Once the doctor releases her, I'll give all three of you a call. We'll work something out."

Ted's mouth opened in a show of outrage. "But what if she escapes again?"

"She won't." Jack aimed a warning glare at her. "Now it's time for you all to leave so she can get some rest."

"But we have orders to take her back," Margaret protested.

Jack put his hands on his hips. "I'm the sheriff here. Hate to state the obvious, but I'm in charge, and the only way I'll release her to you is if that order has been signed by the governor or God. Since it isn't, you're leaving."

"We'll be back," Ted threatened, and he caught Margaret's arm and ushered her out of the room. The door swished closed behind them.

Her brother stayed put.

"I won't be so easily turned away," Sean commented. "We need to figure out what happens next." He didn't wait for them to answer. "My suggestion is to transfer you to another hospital. Maybe one out of state where you can get expert care and won't be under the prying eyes of small-town gossips."

"Gossips?" Alana repeated. "Sean, that's the least of my problems."

"Maybe. But it could be a big problem when word gets out that you might have taken a trip over the cuckoo's nest. Think of your business. Of your clients, who also happen to be mine. You won't keep those clients for long if they think they're dealing with a lunatic."

Sheez. He just didn't get it. "My jewelry designs don't mean much now."

"You say that, but while you've been gone, I've managed to sell nearly every piece you ever designed. To the *right* people. You've won awards, Alana, and if you're smart, you'll use your God-given talent to build on the business reputation I've boosted for you."

Alana couldn't help it. She laughed, even though she was not amused by any of this conversation. "For the past eight months, I've had my life and my son taken from me. If you've had any part in that, I'll never forgive you."

Sean spared her a final glance and looked at Jack. "When will she be well enough to travel?"

"Don't know. You'd have to ask Dr. Bartolo about that."

Sean apparently took that suggestion as gospel. Without so much as mumbling a goodbye, he turned and left.

Alana stood there, looking at the door, and trying to make sense of what'd just happened. Maybe, just maybe she was in the middle of a nightmare, and she would soon wake up to her son and her life. But the look in Jack's eyes confirmed that this was her reality.

"No matter what Dr. Bartolo says, I'm not going with Sean," Alana insisted.

Jack nodded, walked closer and caught her arm. It took Alana a moment to realize why he'd done that, and then she noticed she was shaking. Not just trembling. Actually shaking. He eased her into a sitting position on the bed and put his palm on her forehead.

"Is the fever back?" she asked. Part of her hoped it was because that would be an easy explanation, but she also needed to get well so she could stop whatever was about to happen to her.

"You're not hot."

She was punchy and ready to burst into tears. "I don't think I've ever been so happy to hear a man say that to me."

The corner of his mouth lifted, and it changed his face. He looked even better than he usually did. Her son probably saw a lot of those smiles, and it made her wonder what kind of father Jack had been.

"I haven't thanked you," she said. Best to keep talking because she was afraid if she stopped that she'd fall apart. "For saving my life. For taking in my son. If you hadn't, Sean would have let him become a ward of the court. God knows what would have happened to him."

Jack just stared at her. "I don't need your thanks for taking Joey."

She'd jabbed at the wound again. She'd reminded him they were on opposite sides of a very important issue. "You're right. I'm sorry."

"I don't want your apology, either." He frowned. Cursed. Squeezed his eyes shut for a second and groaned. "Yeah, I'm taking shots at you only minutes after that tornado trio came barreling in through here and tried to tear you to pieces. But the truth is, I don't want to feel anything for you, Alana. Especially concern."

Concern. Well, at least he wasn't feeling this crazy physical attraction. "I could use some concern. And some help. Jack, I'm scared, and I know I shouldn't be admitting that to you. I should be trying to bluff you into thinking I'm strong enough to fight for custody."

He looked at her. Alana expected him to continue to snap at her. After all, she was as much of a threat to him as he was to her. But he didn't.

Jack reached out, put his fingers beneath her chin and lifted it. It wasn't a hug, but it was as close to a comforting gesture as she could have hoped for.

"Careful. I have a virus, remember?" she whispered.

"Yeah, I remember. Just don't breathe on me."

Despite the grumbled warning, his touch was warm. Welcoming. And Alana didn't back away. She sat there and took everything he was offering.

Until there was a sharp rap at the door.

"Yeah?" he called out, and moved his hand. He moved his feet, too, and walked away from her.

The deputy opened the door and stuck in his head. "Just got a call about that commitment order. Thought you'd want to know."

Jack glanced at her, probably debating if this was news he wanted to hear in private.

"If this is about me, I have a right to hear it, too," Alana reminded him.

Jack seemed to consider that and then gave his deputy the nod.

"I checked out the judge, Marvin Pierce. I doubt he signed anything. The guy's been dead and buried for two years now."

Alana's heart began to race. Finally, there was some proof that she'd been railroaded, but that only created more questions.

"So, if he's dead, who signed the order that imprisoned me?" she asked.

The deputy shook his head. "Don't know that, *yet*. It could be a paperwork snafu of some kind. Maybe someone typed in the wrong judge's name when the file was logged into the computer."

That put a slight dent in the hope she'd just felt.

"Let me know as soon as you hear anything else," Jack instructed.

Reyes assured him that he would, and he shut the door.

Alana let out the breath she'd been holding. And then she studied Jack's expression. He didn't look as surprised and vindicated as she felt. "You suspected it might be a suspicious signature on those commitment papers?"

"I considered it." He paused and looked as if he wanted to be anywhere but there. "With all the other things that have happened, it'd be foolish for me not to be skeptical. Your unexplained departure from the hospital eight months ago. The date-rape drug Dr. Bartolo found in your blood. The incident in the alley last night, and Ted's strange way of trying to recapture you."

She continued to study that intense expression. "You're beginning to believe me."

He shrugged. Then nodded. Then shook his head. "I don't want to believe you, but I don't see how all of this could be aboveboard. Something's wrong. Still, that doesn't mean it's all wrong. The commitment papers could have been legal," he added.

In some small way, he believed her. And that meant he might help her.

Alana pushed harder and decided to ask for what she wanted most from him. "I need to see my son, Jack. *Please.*"

She sat there, waiting, and it seemed like an eternity before he finally nodded. "I'll let you see him. But there are some rules."

Alana silently cheered. She was willing to do what he asked. "Anything."

"You won't leave the hospital until the doctor releases you. No more attempts to escape."

"Agreed." Besides, there was no place she wanted to be other than with her son.

"I'll bring Joey here for a short visit. I don't want you holding him because of the virus."

That would be hard, but she wouldn't do anything to put Joey at risk. "What else?"

Jack looked her straight in the eye. "You won't take him from me."

She could have sworn that her heart stopped. "I can't agree to that."

"I mean, you won't do anything about the custody issue, not until I've discovered what the heck is going on."

"Sean probably set up that phony Sauder institution. He's the one who's behind all of this."

"Maybe. But until I have solid proof of that, I want you to promise me that you won't challenge me for custody. I can't handle that kind of distraction when I'm trying to work on this case."

Because she had no choice, she nodded. "But you know that eventually I *will* challenge you. I'll do whatever it takes to get him back."

"I know. And I'll do whatever it takes to stop you."

So they were at a stalemate. Well, sort of. Jack had the power. He had physical custody of her son. "Will you still bring Joey to see me?"

"Yes." Judging from the set of his jaw, it'd taken a lot for him to say that. "But I'm warning you, Alana, if you try to escape or try to pull anything funny, the visit is off. No more playing nice."

She had no intention of going anywhere. After the emotional firestorm she'd just endured, Alana felt drained and raw. But she also felt hope. Soon, she'd get to see her son up close. He would be in the same room with her.

This would be the beginning.

She'd follow Jack's rules. She wouldn't try to escape. And she wouldn't do anything to break this tenuous, temporary agreement.

"So, how soon can I see him?" she asked.

He checked his watch, rubbed his eyes and mumbled

something. "Aunt Tessie's heading back to the ranch. I'll give her a call and have her return."

"You mean now?"

"Now," he verified. He headed for the door and delivered the rest of what he had to say to her from over his shoulder. "Just don't make me regret it."

Alana couldn't promise that she would be on her best behavior. She couldn't speak. Soon, she would get her own version of a miracle.

She'd get to see her son.

Alana thought of the day she'd learned she was going to have a child. Even though the pregnancy wasn't planned, she'd been thrilled. But not Neil. He hadn't wanted children, and the pregnancy had ended their relationship. Good riddance, was what Alana thought at the time. She still felt that way now. Neil was dead, out of the picture.

But not Jack.

Jack had stepped up to raise a stranger's child. He'd prevented her son from going into foster care. And now it was all those good deeds that she'd have to challenge if she wanted custody. Which she did. But then, Alana glanced around the hospital room and considered her predicament. She wasn't exactly in a good place to be fighting for her child, even though that's exactly what she had to do.

Since she was still feeling light-headed, Alana lay back on the bed. No one had brought her clothes yet, so that meant she'd meet her son while she was wearing a hospital gown. Since Joey was only eight months old, he wouldn't notice. She, on the other hand, would commit every little detail about him to memory.

The door flew open. Her heart jumped. But she didn't even have time to make it off the bed before someone turned off the overhead light.

"Jack?" she called out. She was about to ask why he'd done that, but a hand slid over her mouth.

Her instinct was to scream, but the rough hand prevented that. Adrenaline ripped through her. Everything sped up. Her heart. Her breathing. The need to fight and stop whatever was happening to her.

God, what was happening?

"Make a sound, and you'll die right here," someone said. A man.

A stranger's voice.

At least she thought he was a stranger. It was hard to tell—his voice was hoarse and whispered.

"What do you want?" she asked, her own voice muffled beneath his hand. He wore a latex glove.

"You're coming with me," he insisted.

She was about to assure him that she wasn't, but then she felt a sharp jab in her left arm. A shot. He'd given her some kind of injection.

Alana shoved at him, but whoever he was, he was strong. He latched on to her as if she were a rag doll and picked her up from the bed. He forced her to stand. She was weak and dizzy, and he trapped her into the crook of his left arm. Imprisoning her.

"We're leaving," he said in a growl, "and if you don't cooperate, I'll take your son instead of you."

Oh, God. He couldn't hurt Joey. She couldn't let that happen. But how could she stop him?

How?

She forced herself to stay calm. That wasn't easy to

do when her son's life was at stake. Still, she had to come up with some way to prevent him from taking her. Alana didn't know who this man was or what he wanted, but she figured he was taking her to another private mental institution.

And this time, she might not escape.

Moving almost soundlessly, the man carried her to the door and peeked out. Unlike her room, the hall was well lit, and she got a good look at her attacker. Tall, dark haired. His faced was pocked with acne scars. She'd never seen him before. So why was he doing this? Was he working for someone who wanted her back under lock and key?

She was being kidnapped.

Or worse.

He could murder her.

Alana saw someone at the other end of the hall. The person's back was to them. She opened her mouth to call out, but her mouth was numb.

So was the rest of her.

Whatever drug he'd given her had acted fast, and she feared she would soon lose consciousness. If that happened, she wouldn't be able to put up a fight, and even though there were lots of people in the hospital, he might be able to get her out of there without anyone noticing.

Knowing she had to do something, she tried to ram her elbow into his stomach. That didn't work, either. And even though she fought the numbness and the haze, she knew the exact moment she failed.

Alana went limp, and the man scooped her into his arms. The last thing she saw was the bloodred exit sign before everything faded to black.

Chapter Six

What the heck was he doing?

Jack stopped just outside the doors of the hospital entrance and went through everything that'd just happened with Alana.

He cursed again.

Why had he agreed to let Alana see Joey? Why?

Legally, he was Joey's father. Legally, he could control when and if Alana saw him. Of course, he couldn't control that forever. She'd soon file a petition to regain her parental rights. And eventually if she could prove she'd been kidnapped and that she was sane, she would get at least joint custody.

He might lose his son altogether.

That was one of the reasons he'd agreed to let Alana see the baby—Jack had hoped to keep things as amicable as possible between them. Another reason was the blasted compassion he kept feeling for her. He was a sucker for a damsel in distress, and Alana had *damsel* written all over her.

He'd gotten her reassurance that she wouldn't try to escape. Not that she would at this point. If the court order that had put her in the institution wasn't real, and she obviously thought it wasn't, then she probably was already planning her next move to get her son back. Heck, she might be talking to her attorney right now.

And here he had been about to deliver Joey to her.

That wouldn't make her less committed to getting custody. It would cause her to leap at it.

Jack didn't think she'd consider his feelings or think of him with compassion. Nor would she let attraction play into it. No. She'd come after him with a legal team and a lot of money to back up her custody fight.

He needed to have another chat with Alana before he allowed her to see Joey.

Jack turned around, the doors swished open and he retraced his steps through the lobby. Best to get this conversation out of the way. Several people greeted him, but Jack didn't stop, didn't slow down. He went straight for Alana's room.

The door was ajar.

He'd shut it only minutes earlier. He was sure of it. Of course, that wasn't enough reason for concern since this was a hospital where doctors and nurses came and went all the time. Jack peered into the room and spotted the empty bed.

"Alana?" he called out.

Nothing.

He shoved the door wide open and looked around. There was no sign of her. He checked the bathroom, but she wasn't there, either.

Damn. Had she escaped after promising him that she would stay put?

Furious that he'd believed her, he went back into the

hall and saw Dr. Bartolo coming out of one of the other rooms.

"Where's Alana?" Jack asked.

The doctor lifted his shoulder. "She's not in her room?"

Jack cursed again. He'd only left her five or six minutes ago, and he'd been certain that she would sit there and wait for him to return with Joey.

Which is exactly what she would have done.

He stopped and considered that. Alana might have an overwhelming need to escape so she wouldn't be returned to the mental institution, but he was betting that need was paltry compared to the desire to see her son.

And that meant something was wrong.

He pulled out his cell phone and called his deputy. Reyes answered on the first ring. "I need you back at the hospital. Especially the parking lot. We might have a situation with Alana Davis."

"What's the problem?"

"I have a bad feeling her brother might have decided to force her to go with him."

He shoved his phone back into his pocket so his hands would be free. In case of what, he didn't know. Five minutes wasn't that long for Sean to have gotten her out of there, especially if Alana was trying to fight him off, which she would be doing.

They might still be in the building.

But they wouldn't be for long.

Jack glanced around and spotted the nearest exit. It was at the end of the corridor and led to a waiting room. It was usually a busy place, so he looked in the opposite direction. At the emergency exit. Not much foot traffic there, and it led directly to the parking lot.

Oh, man. That bad feeling got a lot worse.

He raced toward the exit and threw open the door. The hot, muggy air engulfed him. So did his concerns as he picked through the sea of cars and saw something he didn't want to see.

Alana.

A big, hulking guy was in the process of cramming her into the backseat of a tan four-door Ford.

Jack drew his gun and barreled down the steps. The position put him at ground level. He could still see the man, but there was a row of cars in between them.

"Sheriff Jack Whitley," he called out to identify himself. "Don't move."

The man practically threw Alana onto the seat and reached for something. The handle on the driver's-side door. Hell.

He wasn't going to stop.

"Rethink that," Jack yelled. "Because I'll shoot. You're not leaving with her."

The man froze and eased his hands into the air. Surrendering. Thank God. Jack didn't want a shoot-out in the hospital parking lot where Alana or an innocent bystander could be hurt. The man didn't seem to be armed. At least there wasn't a weapon visible in either of his hands. However, that didn't mean he didn't have one hidden inside his bulky shirt and jeans.

"Who are you?" Jack demanded.

With his gun ready and aimed, he started toward the Ford. He could see Alana, but she didn't appear to be conscious. Maybe that's why she wasn't moving.

Hopefully, it wasn't something more serious.

He didn't take the time to blame himself for not realizing she was at risk. But he would do that later. After he'd stopped the kidnapping or whatever the heck this was.

"Who are you?" Jack repeated when the guy didn't say a word.

But Jack had hardly finished the question when the man dropped to the ground. He was fast, a blur literally jumping down out of sight.

Jack's body was already primed for a fight, and that caused his adrenaline to soar. He didn't fire. He didn't want to risk hitting Alana. Plus, if the guy was unarmed, then he needed to try to apprehend him first. He might be able to get some answers from him about what was going on.

Jack heard the man was shuffling around. Just in case he was trying to grab Alana from the car, Jack went closer, keeping his own steps light so he could hear what was happening. The shuffling continued, and by the time Jack reached the Ford, the guy wasn't anywhere in sight.

Jack fired his gaze all around the parking lot. Other than the vehicles, there weren't any places to hide. No trees or shrubs. Just a half dozen light poles. While he was looking, he tried to see if he could spot Reyes. He'd told his deputy to head to the parking lot, and Jack knew that Reyes wouldn't let him down.

While he watched for a possible ambush, Jack reached in the car and put her fingers to Alana's neck. She had a pulse. That was the good news. But she wasn't moving, and her color wasn't good. There was a dab of blood of her left arm that looked to be the site of an injection. The guy had drugged her with God knows what, and she might need medical attention.

"Don't make this hard on yourself," Jack called out

to the man. He needed to get this guy under control so he could see to Alana.

Jack eased away from the car and repositioned himself so he could do a visual search. He couldn't go far from the Ford. He couldn't risk the would-be kidnapper doubling back, getting into the car and driving away.

"What's going on?" he heard Reyes yell. Judging from the sound of his voice, the deputy was behind him.

Jack was about to give Reyes a brief description of the perp, but the next sound he heard had him cursing.

It was the sound of a car engine.

Jack turned, reaiming his weapon. It was already too late to respond. At the far end of the parking lot, a dark green car pulled out. The driver slammed on the accelerator, causing the tires to squeal over the concrete surface.

The car sped away.

"Follow him," Jack called out to Reyes, who was already sprinting across the parking lot to get the cruiser he'd left out front. "And call for backup."

That would mean bringing in Kirby Ward, the night deputy, but Jack didn't have a choice. He didn't want Reyes to do this on his own, and he couldn't leave Alana.

While keeping watch, Jack grabbed his cell phone and pressed in the numbers for the hospital dispatch. "I need a doctor in the parking lot *now!*"

He moved closer to Alana and touched her face, hoping it would wake her. Alana stirred, trying to open her eyes, but the attempt wasn't successful.

Alana mumbled something he couldn't understand,

but Jack hoped she could tell him the identity of the man who'd just sped away. If they knew that, then he could figure out who was responsible for this. Someone wanted her away from the hospital, fast, and to accomplish that they'd been willing to risk a kidnapping in broad daylight.

That gave him two bits of critical information.

The person behind this was desperate. And he or she wanted Alana alive. Because if the kidnapper had been able to drug her, he could just as easily have made it a lethal dose. She could be dead by now. But instead, he'd risked taking her through the hospital to a car.

Desperate all right.

And usually when desperation was that huge, it meant this had to do with love or money. Since her brother, Sean, was now at the top of his list of suspects, it could be both.

Sean could have paid the man to take Alana. Why, was the next question. Jack swore he'd find the answer to that soon.

Dr. Bartolo came out of the hospital. He didn't look like a man with fire under his feet, so Jack yelled, "Alana's unconscious. I'm pretty sure somebody drugged her and then tried to kidnap her. She needs help."

That got the doc moving a little faster, but Jack didn't like the lack of urgency. Mercy. What was wrong with the man? Just because Alana was Joey's birth mother, Jack didn't want the town to square off against her.

She had enough enemies.

Dr. Bartolo finally made it to them, and like Jack, the first thing he did was check her pulse. Then he lifted her right eyelid and looked at her pupil. "Yes, she's been drugged. Any idea what she was given?"

"No. The guy who tried to take her didn't say a word."

"Hmmm." The doctor reached for his phone. "I'll have the medics bring out a gurney. She doesn't appear to be injured but better safe than sorry."

Jack couldn't agree more.

The hospital wasn't safe, and he didn't have the manpower to provide round-the-clock protection for her. Willow Ridge was a small town with just him and two deputies. Jack had often pulled double and even triple shifts.

Now he was going to have to take it one step further.

He'd have to take Alana in his protective custody.

Maybe then he could request assistance from the Texas Rangers. Or convince the city council to pay for a bodyguard service or a temporary deputy. But for now, the only solution he could see was to take her to the ranch.

Where she'd see Joey.

It wasn't his first choice. Or even his second. Heck, it wasn't even on the list. But it was his only choice.

He couldn't let her get hurt. He couldn't let that kidnapper come after her again.

"Joey," Alana mumbled.

Jack leaned over her. "He's not here."

Frantically, she shook her head and tried to say something. What, was anyone's guess.

"You're safe now," Jack told her, and to try to reassure her of that, he touched her arm with his fingertips. Rubbed gently. "We'll get you inside, and the doctor will examine you."

She shook her head again, and her face twisted as if she were in pain. "Joey."

It was her hysterical tone and expression that grabbed his attention. "What about him?"

"That man…the kidnapper…he threatened me. He said if I didn't go with him, he'd take Joey."

Jack's heart dropped.

Not this.

Please, God, not this.

"See to Alana," Jack instructed the doctor. And he practically ripped the phone from his pocket. He forced himself to stay calm. Which was impossible. But somehow he managed to stab in the numbers without breaking his cell.

"I think I lost him," Reyes announced when he answered the call.

That didn't get Jack's heart back in his chest, and it kicked up his adrenaline. "Get to the ranch," Jack ordered. He started to sprint toward his car. "I'll meet you there."

"What's wrong?" Reyes asked.

Jack almost hated to say the words aloud. Because the words were a father's nightmare. "The kidnapper's going after Joey."

Chapter Seven

Alana forced open her eyes. She was inside the hospital again. In the E.R. That in itself was enough to cause her to panic, but that particular panic was nothing compared to what she remembered.

The kidnapper had threatened Joey.

She pushed away the hands that were trying to examine her. Dr. Bartolo's hands, she realized.

"Just relax," he insisted. "You're okay."

No. She wasn't. She wouldn't be okay until she stopped that monster from taking her son.

"Joey," she said. Alana sat up and quickly tried to get her bearings. She was dizzy and weak, but that wouldn't prevent her from leaving.

"Jack's already on the way to the ranch," the doctor explained. "I'm sure he'll call the moment he gets there and confirms that all is well."

But everything might not be. The kidnapper's threat was clear. He would use Joey as leverage to get her to cooperate, and Jack might need help.

Alana took a deep breath, hoping it would clear her head, and she got up from the gurney.

"I wouldn't advise that," the doctor warned.

She ignored him and looked around for a pair of shoes or a robe. There was nothing like that in the ER, so that meant she would have to wear just the gown she had on. She started for the door.

Dr. Bartolo caught her arm. She didn't trust him, didn't know the reason for the distrust, and hated that if he hadn't caught her, she would probably have fallen flat on her face.

"Jack's not going to let anything happen to that little boy," the doctor assured her.

He led her back to the gurney. He was right about Jack and she honestly couldn't stand on her own, so Alana had no choice but to sit down. Maybe after a minute or two, she could think straight and figure out how she could help Jack.

"I took a blood sample," the doctor continued. "It'll tell me what kind of drug you were given."

She glanced down at the injection site on her arm. It was a reminder of just what this man was willing to do to kidnap her. He wouldn't be any less ruthless with her child.

"You got a good look at the man who did this?" Dr. Bartolo asked.

Had she? Yes. She had. Alana clearly remembered his face. That was something at least. She'd be able to give a detailed description to Jack. Of course, it was possible that Jack already had an up-close and personal view of the kidnapper since the man might have driven straight to the ranch.

"I need to talk to Jack," she said. "I need to find out what's going on."

She was about to get up again, but she heard the footsteps, looked up and saw Jack. His breath was fast, and there was sweat on his face.

"Where's Joey?" she asked, almost too afraid to hear the answer.

"He's okay."

Alana's heart beat even faster. She was relieved, but that wasn't relief she saw in Jack's expression. "Where is he?"

"Here, at the hospital. Aunt Tessie hadn't gone back to the ranch yet. When I called her, they were at the grocery store, so I went over and got them." Jack looked at the doctor. "How soon before she can leave?"

Dr. Bartolo volleyed glances between them. "I take it you want her out of here?"

"Immediately. We weren't able to find the guy who did this. Reyes is still out looking for him, and the Rangers are sending someone down to assist with the search. But for now, I can't guard Joey and Alana if they're in two separate places."

That got Alana on her feet again. "What are you going to do?"

"I'm taking you, Joey and Tessie to my office. There's a small break room with a sofa sleeper. It's pretty sparse, but you'll have to use that until I can make other arrangements."

She didn't care about sparse. Her only requirement was that it be safe for her son. "And Joey will be there, too?"

Jack spared her a glance, but he didn't look directly at her. His body was tense and tight. His chest, still pumping. "I don't have a choice. Joey will be there."

How ironic. The threat of imminent danger would be

the reason she could see her son. But Alana gladly would have postponed that meeting if she could be guaranteed that this man wouldn't go after Joey.

"She'll probably be woozy for a while," the doctor said. "She should rest. This sounds like the start of big mother and child reunion, but my advice is for her not to hold Joey until we're sure this virus has run its course."

Even that didn't dampen Alana's spirits. For now, she would be satisfied with simply meeting the child she'd given birth to.

"Bring her back tomorrow for a checkup," the doctor added.

"Will do." Jack went to her and took her by the arm. He pulled the blanket from the gurney and wrapped it around her like a cape. "Once things have settled, I'll see about getting you some clothes."

Settled. Heaven knows when that would be. "Thank you for this, Jack."

He didn't answer. He got her moving. There was a sense of urgency and unease in his every step.

Her feelings mirrored his. She was afraid, but the fear lifted in a snap when Jack and she walked out of the ER and into the adjacent waiting room. His aunt Tessie was there.

She was holding Joey, just a few feet away.

So close that Alana could practically touch him.

The little boy was a good antidote for the drug still left in her body. Suddenly, she didn't feel hazy. Every inch of her was on alert, and she took in as many details as she could. She'd only gotten a glimpse of him earlier, and he hadn't been nearly this close to her. She wanted to hold on to this moment forever.

He was bigger than she'd imagined he would be, and Jack had been right about the eye color. Blue, an identical shade to hers. His face was round with a flash of rosy color in his cheeks, and that beautiful face was framed with soft brown hair that was thin and spiky.

He was precious.

Joey looked at her with those now suspicious blue eyes and wound his arms tighter around Tessie's neck. He didn't cry, but he certainly wasn't sending her any welcoming signals. But that didn't matter. He would get to know her.

And she would get to know him.

"Alana," Tessie greeted. There was a hint of anger in her eyes and more than a little fear and concern.

Alana understood why. This woman had been a mother figure to Joey. She'd helped Jack raise him, and she would see Alana as a threat.

"Tessie," she greeted back. "I remember you brought me Christmas dinner after I gave birth to Joey. You were kind to me, and I appreciate that."

"We need to go," Jack said, voiding the rest of the polite conversation. It wasn't the time for it, anyway. After all, the kidnapper could return to try to make good on his threat to take Joey.

"My car's right in front of the hospital," Jack explained as he led them in that direction. "We'll do this as fast as we can. Alana, you get in the front with me. Tessie and Joey will take the back since that's where his infant seat is. If you see anything of concern, let me know immediately."

Concern.

Translation: danger.

Alana wanted to take her son and shelter him in her arms, but she knew that wouldn't be wise. She was still light-headed from the effects of the drug. Plus, there was the virus.

Jack didn't waste any time. The moment the front doors swished open, he drew his weapon and looped his left arm around Tessie. The maneuver sandwiched Joey between the two, and they hurried to the black SUV. Alana got in as quickly as she could, and the moment that Tessie had Joey strapped into the seat, Jack drove away.

Alana kept watch in the side mirror, to make sure no one was following them. Jack did the same. His gaze darted all around them. From the backseat, she could hear Tessie talking softly to Joey. The woman was trying to reassure him that all was well, but he had to be aware of the increased tension.

But hopefully not the danger.

"I'm sorry this is happening," Alana said to Jack.

He didn't look at her. He didn't answer her.

"Maybe this man is responsible for what happened eight months ago," she added, talking more to herself than Jack.

"Maybe." But it didn't sound as if he believed that. "I'll check the surveillance video again, but I don't remember seeing him."

Still monitoring their surroundings, he took the turn toward Main Street. There was only a trickle of traffic here, and the two-lane road was practically rural since the hospital was positioned on the outskirts of town.

"He wanted you alive," Jack continued. "So that means he had ransom or some other form of reward in mind."

"He knew I had a son. He said 'if you don't cooperate, I'll take your son instead of you.'"

Because she needed reassurance that he was okay, she glanced over her shoulder at Joey. Tessie was singing him a song, and he was smiling at her.

When they reached Main Street, Jack pulled into the small parking lot of the sheriff's office and drove to the back. There was a door labeled Emergency Exit, and it had a sign that instructed visitors to enter through the front. Jack parked as close to the door as possible, unlocked it and started the transfer. He had them all inside within seconds.

"Take Joey to my office," Jack instructed Tessie. He relocked the emergency exit and activated a security alarm. "The break room's through here."

In the opposite direction as his office.

She would be under the same roof as Joey, but Jack didn't intend to let her spend time with him. Still, it wasn't far. Just on the other side of the hall.

The break room was indeed sparse. It had a sofa and a small table with two chairs. There was a coffeepot and various packs of crackers and chips on the narrow counter beneath two white-painted cabinets. A miniature brown fridge hummed in the corner.

Jack opened a closet and pulled out a pillow and a patchwork quilt. "Dr. Bartolo said you should rest," he reminded her. He also grabbed a pair of black sweatpants and a man's white button shirt that was dangling on a hanger. "The doors are all locked. No one's going to get in without me knowing it. It's safe here."

"Rest," she repeated, knowing that wasn't going to happen. "I can give you my statement now. Or whatever you call it. I'll do whatever you need me to do to help find this man."

He tossed the bedding onto the sofa and handed her the clothes. He also took a plastic bag from the top of the closet. "For now, I need you to rest. Oh, and I need that hospital gown. It might have some DNA or trace that could lead us to the kidnapper."

She took the clothes from him, mumbled a thanks and motioned for him to turn around. He did. And Alana caught the counter so she could keep her balance while she stepped into the pants. They were several sizes too large for her, but anything was better than the open-back hospital gown. She pulled it off, placed it next to the coffeepot and slipped on the shirt. It, too, was big and the bottom hit her at midthigh.

These must be Jack's clothes.

The shirt carried his scent.

"Now rest," Jack insisted. He checked over his shoulder as she was managing the last button.

Alana didn't budge. She couldn't. She was afraid if she sat, she'd fall back asleep. The drug the kidnapper had given her was still in her system, and she was lightheaded. She didn't want to feel this way. She wanted to be able to help Jack keep Joey safe, and for that to happen she had to stay awake.

Jack huffed, riled that she wasn't cooperating. He walked to her, took her gown and stuffed it into the plastic bag. He laid it aside on the counter and caught her arm. He tugged her toward the sofa, but Alana stayed put.

"I need to help. I need to do something," she insisted.

"You've done enough." He was angry.

It took her a moment to fight through the fog in her

head and study his expression. He didn't turn away. Jack just stood there and stared at her.

And then it hit her.

"Oh, God. I'm sorry." She pressed her fingertips to her mouth to stop it from trembling. "I'm so sorry."

"Don't," he warned. And it was indeed a warning. He wasn't pleased about this situation—or about her—and she suddenly understood why. It wasn't just the fact that she would be so close to her son.

It was because she'd brought this danger to Joey.

She hadn't meant to do that. Her escape from the house in the woods had been so frightening. So chaotic. She hadn't had time to think. If she had, if she'd realized there was real danger, she wouldn't have come anywhere near her son. Though she had no idea what she would have done.

Her life was spiraling out of control, and she didn't know what to do to make it stop.

Alana started to tremble. Not just her mouth as she tried to speak. But her entire body. And she had no choice but to try to get to the sofa. She had to sit after all.

"I didn't know that coming here would put Joey in danger," she said. "I swear, I didn't know." Mercy, she sounded hysterical and was very close to it. How could she have done this to her son?

Jack opened his mouth, closed it and then cursed under his breath. His grip tightened around her arm, and he physically sat her on the sofa.

"Look, I want to be angry with you. I'm not especially happy you're here." He dropped down beside her and groaned. "But I also know you wouldn't intentionally endanger Joey."

That admission was more than she could have hoped for, and the relief had an instant effect. It was as if her muscles suddenly had permission to unknot. She went limp, and her head landed against Jack's shoulder. Alana didn't let it stay there. She started to move.

But Jack caught her again.

He slid his arm around her and pulled closer to him.

"I'm scared," she admitted.

"Me, too." That was all he said for several moments. "I'm usually objective about my job. I do what I have to do to keep the peace in this town. But Joey's not the job. I don't how it happened, but eight months ago when I held him in my arms, he became my son."

She blinked back tears. "I wish he were yours." Alana felt both of them go stiff. She didn't know who was more surprised with her admission: Jack or her. "I mean, uh, you're a better man than his biological father."

Jack turned his head. He snared her gaze and stared at her. Something changed between them. Maybe the air. Maybe it was all in her head. But she saw something in his eyes that she thought she hadn't seen before.

Solidarity.

They were on the same side, at least when it came to Joey. That was a powerful union. She was Joey's mother, and Jack was his father in every way that counted. In that moment, Alana knew she would have to make concessions. She couldn't cut Jack out of Joey's life.

She didn't want to.

Her son deserved a father like Jack.

"We'll work this out," Alana promised. And she meant it.

Something else went through his eyes. Emotions that she tried to catalog. Gratitude, maybe. Relief, definitely. At that point, it probably would have been a good idea for her to look away, but she didn't.

There was a sense of everything slowing down. And getting warmer.

Not warmer, she amended.

Hotter.

Alana recognized the feelings that trickled through her. This was attraction. Basic. Human.

Strong.

Jack shook his head, as if to clear it. But she saw the heat in his eyes, as well. Now he would back off. He'd say something to explain this all away, something to do with the near life-and-death experience she'd just had.

But that didn't happen, either.

Jack leaned in, lowered his head. His breath brushed over her mouth.

The jolt was sharp and intense. For a moment she thought it was static electricity, but this wasn't painful. This was some kind of pleasure that was so intense, it was downright scary. It slid through every inch of her.

Alana pulled back and drew in a sharp breath.

"Yeah," he said. "That was stupid."

"The craziness got to us," she heard herself say. Now she was the one trying to explain what'd happened. Great. She didn't know what'd happened. Heck, it wasn't even a kiss.

"Alana..." His tone was apologetic, but he waved it off and stood. He went to the other side of the room, as far away from her as he could get without leaving. Which she figured he would do next.

"Alana..." This time, he was disgusted with himself.

She stood, as well. "Jack..." She winced because they were just saying each other's names as if they'd both turned brainless. "I hope you don't get sick."

Alana winced again at the idiotic comment. At her schoolgirl nerves. At the fact that Jack was the last man she should be lusting after.

Wasn't he?

Hot raging hormones had a way of doling out excuses, and she had a whopper. Since Jack and she both had Joey's best interest at heart, it seemed logical that they would feel a closeness. After all, he was a man and she was a woman. They were both single.

As if he could read her mind, Jack shook his head. "We already have too much to work out." His words were calm, void of any emotion.

And it was true.

Less than an hour earlier, someone had tried to kidnap her. The person might try again. Or might even go after Joey. This was not the time or place for hot raging hormones.

She nodded, told her body to knock it off and sank back onto the sofa. She needed to sleep off the kidnapper's drug. Just a short nap. And then maybe she could watch Joey from a distance. But her head had barely hit the pillow when there was a sharp rap.

"Someone's at the front door," Jack informed her.

The kidnapper. God, had he returned? She jumped up from the sofa again and was about to run to Joey.

"A kidnapper probably wouldn't knock first," Jack reminded her. He walked out, heading in the direction of the front door.

He was right again. The kidnapper would be a fool to try to come after her while she was in the sheriff's office.

Alana tamped down the fight instinct and cursed the light-headedness that was causing her not to think straight. She went to the doorway of the break room so she could listen. Jack was already out of sight, but she heard when he opened the door.

And she heard him snap, "What the heck do you want now?"

Alana used the wall for support and made her way up the hall, toward the sound of Jack's voice.

It was her brother, Sean.

She rounded the corner just in time to see Sean hand Jack some papers. Jack glanced at the top page and then mumbled some profanity. Alana went closer to see what had caused Jack's reaction.

"This is for your own good," Sean told her.

Her stomach clenched. Whenever her brother said anything like that, it was usually for his own good, not hers.

"What is it?" she asked Jack, dreading the answer. They had enough to face without adding anything else to the mix.

Jack held up his index finger and continued to read the papers. While he did that, Alana decided to deal with her brother.

"Did you send a kidnapper after me?" she asked. She caught the wall for support and waited for his answer.

Sean didn't look particularly surprised or outraged. Only mildly annoyed. "Of course not. Why? Did someone try to kidnap you?"

"Someone did," she assured him, mimicking his annoyed tone. "Someone also had me committed to that Sauder institution by forging the signature of a dead judge. Would you happen to know anything about that?"

"Nothing."

"You're lying." But she couldn't be sure of that at all. Her brother had always been a good liar. And a manipulator. But she had to admit that this seemed extreme even for him. This was a lot of go through for the sake of maintaining appearances.

"I suppose you think I'm lying about that, too?" Sean tipped his head to the papers Jack was still reading.

He was too smug for that to be a bluff. Those papers were obviously trouble.

She went to Jack so she could have a look for herself. "It's a court order," Jack explained. His gaze snapped to Sean's. "How did you manage to get this done so quickly? You only left the hospital about an hour and a half ago."

Sean lifted his hands and stayed smug. "What can I say? I know people who know people. A family friend signed it and faxed it to me."

"And is this judge dead like the other one who signed the original court order?" Jack asked.

"No. He's very much alive and on the bench in San Antonio. He's sympathetic to my family's situation. My sister's well-being in the most important thing in my life right now."

Alana ignored him and tried to read the paper, but dizziness was causing the words to squirm on the page. "What kind of court order is it?" she asked Jack.

The muscles in Jack's jaw went to war with each

other. "It's a commitment order. Until the new judge can interview you and examine your case files, you're to be returned to the mental institution immediately."

Chapter Eight

Jack looked at Alana. What little color she'd had in her cheeks had drained to white. Sean, on the other hand, looked pleased as punch with himself.

Jack wanted to bash the guy in the face.

Since that wasn't an appropriate reaction for a peace officer, he settled for pushing the newly issued commitment papers against Sean's chest. Jack wasn't gentle about it, either, and Sean staggered back a step.

"Please don't make me go," Alana said. Her voice was broken and near panic.

"You're not going anywhere," Jack assured her.

That earned him a raised eyebrow from Sean. "You intend to ignore a judge's order?"

"Damn right, I do." Jack chose his words carefully because one slip, and he could find himself on the wrong side of the law. "Your sister's a witness to an attempted felony—her own kidnapping. And because she's the only person who can identify her attacker, she's in my protective custody."

Alana didn't relax. She eyed Sean to see what he would do next.

Sean waved the papers at them. "I'm not a lawyer, but I don't think a sheriff of Podunkville can ignore a judge's order."

Jack didn't appreciate the insult, but he took some pleasure that his refusal to hand over Alana was causing Sean to lose his cool. "This Podunk sheriff can. Your judge is on the bench in San Antonio. That's Bexar County. He has no jurisdiction here. And Alana's not even a resident of San Antonio. She hasn't lived there in over eight months."

Alana's arm was touching his, and Jack felt her relax a bit. Not Sean, though. His eyes narrowed. "You don't want to make me your enemy."

"Really?" Jack couldn't help himself. Sean was testing his patience. "I don't mind enemies."

"You won't think that way for long," Sean threatened. "I'll get another judge to sign the order. One in this county. And I'll be back." He turned to walk away.

"It'll be a waste of time," Jack commented.

Sean slowly turned around to face him. "What does that mean?"

"It means I know every judge in this county."

A little of Sean's smugness returned. "Yes, I'll bet you do. And not because you're the sheriff. I know what you did to your own father." He paused, smiled. "Does Alana know?"

Jack had to fight to hang on to his composure. "No. It's not pertinent to this case, and neither is the fact you brought it up. If you're trying to undermine me, it won't work. I'm not my father, and I have a solid reputation in this town and in this county. Any judge will agree with me once I tell them why Alana is in my protective custody."

That took care of Sean's smile. He gave Jack one last hard look, and he stormed toward his car.

Alana sagged against him. Jack looped his arm around her to stop her from falling.

"Thank you, again," she whispered. "You seem to be coming to my rescue a lot."

He was surprised and thankful that she didn't ask about his father. "Rescues are part of the job description." Best to keep things light. And after that stupid near kiss, he needed to make her understand that this was the job.

Well, for the most part.

Jack couldn't lie to himself. He'd already tried that and failed. But he couldn't kiss her. Wanting to kiss her was an entirely different matter. He didn't think he could talk his body out of wanting to do that. But he would fight hard not to cross that particular line.

He locked the door and led her back to the break room. On the other side of the hall, he could hear Joey and Tessie. It sounded as if Tessie was reading to him. She'd probably found a kids' book in the small toy chest that Jack kept in the closet in his office.

"Are you okay?" Jack called out to them.

"We're fine," Tessie answered. "What's going on?"

"I'll be over in a minute to explain everything." But first he wanted to get Alana settled and hopefully on her way to a much-needed nap.

"Good. By the way, a fax just came for you," Tessie let him know. "It says urgent on the cover letter."

Alana stopped. "Do you think it's about the man who tried to kidnap me?"

"Maybe." But more likely it was about Alana herself. Reyes had put out a lot of feelers on this case, and the fact that it was marked *urgent* meant he had to deal with it ASAP.

With his arm still looped around Alana, he started for the break room again, but she stopped. "Could I go with you to get the fax?"

"I don't think that's a good idea."

She pushed her hair from her face and sighed. "I won't touch Joey. I just want to look at him."

Of course she'd want to look at her son. The logical part of Jack's brain knew that was a natural reaction. The illogical part wanted Alana in that break room. But he couldn't keep her away for long. Nor was he sure that was even a good idea. For better or worse, Alana was here, in Joey's life, and somehow he had to deal with that and keep his son in the process.

"We'll get the fax, and then we can go to the break room so you can tell me why Sean is so hell-bent on putting you back in a mental institution."

"I can tell you that now." They took it slow walking down the hall. "Sean will say that he's concerned about appearances, and in part, that's true. But the real reason he's doing this is for the money."

Jack figured that would play into this somehow. "How would keeping you locked away get Sean money?"

"We both inherited fifty percent of our parents' jewelry business when they died. It's worth a lot. Millions. Well, it was eight months ago, anyway. Since I've been out of my mind, literally, Sean would have had sole control of the business and the money."

"And you think he wants to keep that control?" Jack asked.

"Oh, yes. Our parents died eight years ago when I

was twenty-one. Sean's six years older than I am, and at that time he had a lot more experience in the business. He had his own contacts. His own way of doing things. He's tried to buy me out numerous times, and every time I've refused. I might not know the business as well as Sean, but I wanted to keep control of my own designs. I knew if Sean bought me out, that wouldn't happen. He tends to go for profit rather than quality."

Jack gave that some thought. "How's the business structured? Do the profits go into one account?"

Alana shook her head. "Two. The profits are split fifty-fifty and deposited into our individual accounts."

Jack made a note to check into Alana's financial records. They might hold some clues as to why this was happening to her.

She paused when they were just a few steps from his office. "I don't want my brother to be guilty of this. I don't want to believe he could choose money over blood."

Neither did he, but Jack had seen it happen too many times to discount Sean as his primary suspect. Besides, he didn't hold a lot of stock with blood. His father was proof of that.

They stopped in the doorway of his office. Tessie was sitting in his chair holding Joey. She was trying to read to him, but Joey had already lost interest in the book. He was squirming and doing his best to get down. Tessie held on, probably because she didn't want Joey trying to crawl in Alana's direction.

When Joey's attention landed on Jack, he stopped squirming. "Da-Da," he babbled. He gave Jack one of those big, priceless grins.

Jack smiled back, went to them and scooped Joey into his arms. He got rewarded with a hug. But Joey's interest was held only for a second. His son's exploring fingers and eyes went straight to the badge clipped onto Jack's belt. Because Jack knew what Joey wanted, he took off the silver star and handed it to him.

Joey beamed and made a few syllables to indicate he had the "toy" he wanted. With Joey now content—for at least a moment or two, anyway—Jack went to the fax machine.

Alana stayed in the doorway, but she had her attention focused on Joey. The little boy spotted her and lifted the badge as if to show her his prize.

"It's shiny, isn't it?" Alana said. There was so much emotion in her voice that Jack worried she was close to crying. However, she blinked back tears.

Joey answered her with more babbles and gave her a smile, as well. Jack knew that was a moment she would remember for the rest of her life.

"Why did you come back?" Tessie asked.

Oh, no. Jack hadn't wanted this conversation to happen now. Not with Alana still woozy from the kidnapper's drug. "It's complicated," Jack explained.

Alana obviously wanted to take that explanation further. "I have no memory of why I left the hospital that night. I don't know what happened, but it must have been extremely serious to make me leave the way I did."

"No memory," Tessie repeated. Jack knew that tone. She was skeptical. But he also knew that his aunt was a fair and reasonable woman. If they learned that Alana hadn't voluntarily walked out eight months ago, then

Tessie would step up and try to make things better—just as she'd done twenty years ago when Jack was a kid.

"I think someone might have drugged me that night," Alana continued. "And threatened Joey, too. There aren't any other reasons that would make me walk out and leave my son behind."

While the women continued to talk, Jack looked at the fax. It was from the Texas Rangers in San Antonio. He read through the two paragraphs. And then read it again. When he finished, he realized that both Tessie and Alana were staring at him, obviously waiting to hear why the fax had been deemed "urgent."

Jack decided to start with the simple item first. "The Rangers did a quick check of the Sauder Facility. Everything about it is bogus."

Alana's breath shuddered. "There's proof?"

He nodded and idly gave Joey a kiss on the forehead when the little boy babbled something. "Everything is fake. The permit for the place. The judge's signature on your commitment papers. The foundation set up to pay your expenses."

"So where did the money come from?" Alana asked.

"They don't know yet." Their gazes met, and he saw in Alana's eyes what was no doubt in his. The money had probably come from Sean. "There are now APBs out on Margaret Vargas and Ted Moore."

Alana nodded and swallowed hard. "They had to be in on this."

"Not necessarily. They could have believed the institution and commitment orders were real. There could even have been phony orders or instructions from a doctor. Still, I want to question them." He glanced at the fax again. "The Rangers want to know the location of the place so they can send a CSI unit through it."

Alana nodded, then huffed. "I don't know the names of the roads, but I think I could take you there."

That's what he was afraid she would say. He wasn't exactly champing at the bit to drive her out to a remote facility where she'd been held prisoner. And he didn't want her to face the stress it would cause. It might not be safe. Whoever was behind this might have the place staked out. The trip could turn into a dangerous trap, and this time the kidnapper might succeed. Still, there could be valuable information inside. Info that would break this case wide open.

"After you've rested, try to draw a map," Jack instructed. Maybe it wouldn't be necessary. Maybe the Rangers would find Margaret and Ted and get them to confess to everything.

This was starting to get beyond complicated.

"Does the name Special Agent Parker Howell mean anything to you?" Jack asked, reading from the second paragraph of the fax.

Her eyes lit up with recognition. "Yes." But just as quickly, her forehead bunched up. "He's an FBI agent. I remember him coming to my office about a year ago. He was investigating the sale of illegally obtained diamonds. I didn't have any information to help him."

He read through the fax again to make sure he hadn't missed something. "And?"

"That was it." She paused. "At least I think it was." Her forehead bunched up even more. "Why?"

"Because he's been trying to locate you. He requested assistance from the Rangers eight months ago when you disappeared. He saw the APB that was put out when you left the Sauder Facility, and he's on his way here to Willow Ridge."

Alana shook her head. "What does he want?"

"The fax doesn't say. I hoped you might know."

"No." Her voice and expression were laced with questions and concerns.

Jack shared those concerns. What did an FBI agent want with Alana? He hoped like the devil that she hadn't been involved in anything illegal.

Then rethought that and decided she wouldn't have done anything illegal. Not voluntarily, anyway.

He cursed.

He was neck-deep in personal involvement here. Much to his disgust, any objectivity he should have about this case was long gone. Alana had been railroaded. End of speculation as to her guilt or innocence. That made him either one perceptive lawman or an idiot.

Yeah. That desire to kiss her had really screwed up things.

"Get some rest," Jack told Alana again. "I'll wake you when Special Agent Howell arrives."

She nodded, but didn't budge. The smile she aimed at Joey was weak from fatigue, but she continued to stare at the baby. "What will happen, Jack? It's not fair to the three of you to be cooped up here with me."

Another thing that had to be worked out. "We'll stay here tonight. I'll have Reyes, my deputy, bring in some cots and supplies. Maybe by morning, we'll have this situation resolved. If not, we'll go to the ranch. It's not quite as secure at this building, but I can get the ranch hands to put together some safety measures."

"And then what?" Alana asked.

"I don't know," he admitted. He hated that he didn't have the answers. His son's safety might be at stake, and that meant he had to do whatever it took to keep Joey out of harm's way.

Jack heard the rattle of the knob on the front door, and he groaned. Hopefully, it wasn't Agent Howell already. He wanted Alana to rest before that meeting. However, the rattle was quickly followed by the sound of someone inserting a key into the lock.

"It's me," Reyes called out a moment later.

Since it was possible that his deputy had the kidnapper in custody, Jack handed Joey to Tessie and went past Alana and into the hall.

Reyes was alone. And the man looked seriously riled.

"He got away," Reyes snarled. Though Jack had already figured that out. "I swear I'll get him, though. Just give me some time."

Jack believed him. He only wished he didn't have his own hands so full that he couldn't do some legwork to track down this guy. "I want his car impounded and searched. There might be something in it to reveal his identity. Run the plates, too. We could get lucky."

"We have to get something from that car. It might be our only source of evidence." Reyes glanced at Alana, reached behind him and locked the door. "The surveillance camera doesn't monitor that end of the parking lot. And since he used the emergency exit to get in and out, there won't be any film of him."

"He wore latex gloves," Alana volunteered.

That caused Reyes to look even more riled.

"I bagged the gown she was wearing." Jack hitched

his thumb to the break room. "It's on the counter. Let me get Alana in there for a nap, and I'll do the paperwork to have it processed."

The phone rang, and while Reyes answered the call at the front desk, Jack walked with Alana to the break room. Maybe this time he'd actually get her into the makeshift bed so she could rest.

Or not, he decided when he heard Reyes ask the caller, "You're sure it's the Sauder institution where Alana Davis was being held?"

Jack and Alana stopped and waited for the conversation to end. Reyes hung up, and in the same motion, he turned and snared Jack's gaze. "We might have gotten a break. The Rangers learned the location of the institution. It's about an hour from here, out in the middle of the sticks. They're headed over there to check it out."

Good. That could indeed be a break, especially since Alana wouldn't have to get anywhere near the place. Between the facility and the kidnapper's car, they might actually find something useful that would lead to the arrest of whoever was responsible.

Jack didn't have time to savor that possibility because from out the window he saw a man making his way to the front door. Tall. About six-two. Rust-brown hair, cut short and efficient. The guy wore a suit.

This was no doubt Special Agent Parker Howell.

The timing sucked, but this could turn out to be yet more good news.

Jack was more than a little uneasy about what a federal agent would want with Alana, especially if this pertained to those illegal diamonds.

Reyes was the one who opened the door, and the visitor immediately made a sweeping glance around the room. His attention landed on Jack. Then Parker looked past Jack at Alana. He flashed a dazzling smile that made Jack even more uncomfortable.

What the heck was going on here? That wasn't the normal greeting of a federal agent working in an official capacity. It was too friendly.

"Alana," the man greeted.

"Agent Parker Howell," she said stiffly. "What can I do for you?"

The dazzling smile faded. "Agent Parker Howell?" he repeated. "Why so formal?" But he didn't wait for an answer. He turned to Jack. "Was Alana hurt? I heard she was attacked at the hospital."

"How'd you hear that?" Jack asked.

"From the Rangers." He stepped inside and walked closer, his attention fastened again to her. "I'm sorry about the attack, Alana. If I'd found you sooner, I might have been able to prevent it. That's why I'm here. To stop anything else from happening to you. I'm here to take you into protective custody."

Jack didn't say a word. He stood back and listened. For now. But Alana wasn't leaving with this man.

"You're too late," she insisted. "I'm already in Sheriff Whitley's custody."

"That was a good temporary measure." He turned to Jack. "And I thank you for helping us out. But the FBI has authority here."

"How do you figure that?" Jack asked.

Agent Howell shrugged as if the answer were obvious. "Because Alana is a federal informant."

Chapter Nine

Alana was too tired and too numb to have an extreme reaction. But, mercy, could her life get any more complicated?

"A federal informant?" Jack asked. It was a challenge.

"Yes." Agent Howell shifted those ice-gray eyes in her direction. "You don't remember?"

"Remember what, exactly?" she asked.

He lifted his shoulder. "Anything about your dealings with the FBI."

She glanced at Jack before she answered. "There are some blank spots in my memory. But I do recall you coming to my office in San Antonio to discuss some diamonds."

"Blood diamonds," the agent calmly provided. He kept his attention on her eyes as if he were examining her. "That's what we discussed that day."

"I remember that part. I also remembering turning down your request for me to become a federal informant."

"You did, at first. But it wasn't just the one visit. I

saw you again Christmas Eve, and we spoke on the phone several times before that. It was during one of those phone conversations when you finally agreed to help us. You don't remember any of that?"

Alana took a moment to try to recall other meetings, but nothing came to mind. Of course, the meetings could have happened. She'd already tried to piece together those last several days before Joey was born, and she had no idea what she'd done or whom she'd spoken to.

"I'm sorry, Agent Howell, but I don't remember," she admitted.

"Parker," he corrected, offering his first name as if they were that familiar with each other. And maybe they were.

Jack caught her when she wobbled a bit. "Did those meetings and conversations have anything to do with what's happening to her now?" he asked.

"Possibly." Without taking his eyes off her, Parker reached into his suit coat pocket and extracted a picture. It was a grainy shot, but the man in the image was still visible. "Is this the person who attacked you at the hospital?"

Alana's breath started to race, and she nodded before she even took the picture from him and brought it closer to her face. Not that she needed a closer look. She'd recognized him after one glimpse. "That's the man."

Jack's grip on her arm got slightly firmer. "Who is he?" he wanted to know.

"Eldon Thatcher."

Reyes crossed the room and looked at the picture, as well. "Can I borrow this? I want to send it out to the sheriffs in the surrounding area. The guy's probably still close, which means we can catch him."

"Be my guest," Parker offered, and Alana handed the picture to the deputy. He took it and disappeared into his office.

"Eldon Thatcher is the one who had the illegal diamonds that he was trying to sell to you." Parker paused. "You really don't remember?"

"Remember what?" she snapped at him. She was very uncomfortable about what she wasn't recalling. And that had a lot to do with the agent in front of her.

Why did she distrust him?

It was the same niggling feeling she'd gotten when she saw Dr. Bartolo. There was just something about both of them that made her uneasy.

Parker took a deep breath. "Eldon Thatcher had these diamonds, and using an alias, he contacted you, hoping you'd buy them despite the lack of paperwork that would prove they were his and not illegally obtained. You got suspicious of him and recorded the conversation. Then you phoned the FBI. We identified the potential seller and asked you to set up a sting operation. We wanted to use your portion of the company to process the sale of the diamonds so we could catch Thatcher."

"And did you catch him?" Jack asked.

"No." Parker had the same look that Reyes had had when he walked in and announced the kidnapper had gotten away. But unlike Reyes's account, something about this didn't sound right.

Alana took a step forward and met Parker's gaze head-on. "Are you saying I agreed to cooperate with this sting operation?"

Parker nodded. "You did."

Alana huffed. "But I was pregnant. Nearly eight

months along. And I would have known this might be dangerous."

Another nod. "You still wanted to do it. Of course, we didn't know it would actually place you in danger. All we asked you to do was to agree to speak with Thatcher again. Not even in person. We wanted you to handle the transaction over the phone. An agent would have stood in for you if you could have arranged a sale to take place on Christmas day." He shrugged. "That didn't happen."

"Why not?" Jack demanded, his voice cutting through the silence.

"Honestly, we don't know. We think someone tipped off Thatcher that Alana was an informant. When I realized what'd happened, I tried to call Alana and warn her, but she wasn't home. Her housekeeper said she'd left unexpectedly. After that, she disappeared."

That filled in a few blanks. *If* he was telling the truth. "Why did I come to Willow Ridge?"

He shook his head. "I don't know. Maybe you realized someone was following you, and you started driving and ended up here."

Because she badly wanted to refute that, Alana squeezed her eyes shut and tried to force herself to remember. It didn't work. There was a huge gap of time missing between that meeting with Parker and Jack pulling her from that frozen creek.

"From what I've heard, you've been through a lot," the agent continued. "We can arrange proper medical care for you. Maybe then your memory will return."

Jack stepped closer to Parker. "Are we back to the protective custody issue now?"

"Yes. Alana has to go with me."

"No. I don't," she said as the exact moment that Jack said, "No, she doesn't."

Parker's eyes widened. "Why would you refuse protection? Alana, you could be in grave danger. Your son, too. Thatcher's a dangerous man."

"Obviously. He came after me at the hospital. Now, why would he do that? Before today, I'd never seen his face. I couldn't identify him."

"Who knows?" Parker lifted his hands, palm up. "He might just be trying to eliminate anyone who could connect him to those diamonds."

"That doesn't make sense," Jack insisted. "If all Thatcher wanted was Alana out of the way, then why didn't he just kill her in the hospital room?"

As chilling as that possibility was, Jack was right.

Parker glanced away. Groaned under his breath. "This sounds gruesome, but he might have wanted to torture her first. As I said, Thatcher is dangerous."

Alana hadn't doubted that for a moment. "I'm not going with you," she informed the agent.

Parker's gaze slashed back to hers. "That could be a fatal mistake."

"Could be," she agreed. But she was going to rely on her instincts here, and her instincts were to trust Jack. Besides, she had no intention of leaving her son.

Parker extracted his business card from his pocket and handed it to her. "All right, then. I'll inform my boss of your decision, but call me if you change your mind." He turned as if to leave, but then stopped. He looked at Jack. "When Thatcher tries to take her again, my advice is shoot to kill. Because he won't stop. He'll keep coming after her until he succeeds."

"I wish he were saying that just to scare me," Alana mumbled as she watched the agent walk away. "But he's probably right about this Eldon Thatcher."

Jack shut the door, locked it and in the same motion he caught her arm and led her in the direction of the break room. "Talk to me about Agent Howell. The meeting with him that you can remember, how did it go?"

"Not well, actually. I told him that as a jewelry maker I got contacted often by sellers who were suspicious. These sellers either had no paperwork to prove ownership of what they were offering, or the paperwork was doubtful at best. That's why I declined Parker's request when he wanted me to set up this particular sting."

"He says you changed your mind." Jack's tone mirrored her own doubts about what the agent had claimed.

Alana sank onto the sofa the moment they made it into the break room. "Why would he lie about something like that?"

"Maybe because he's trying to cover his butt."

Alana shook her head. "What do you mean?"

Jack eased the door shut and motioned for her to lie down. He didn't continue until she complied. She could have sworn her feet and back breathed sighs of relief at the prospect of finally getting some rest. Still, she would have preferred to be in the room with Joey while they worked to find answers about this investigation.

"Parker said the FBI was going to use a stand-in if the deal went down," Jack explained. "When you refused to get involved with the case, he might have used you anyway. He could have had this stand-in pose as you and contact Eldon Thatcher to arrange the sale."

Alana worked her way through that theory. "And maybe something went wrong. Maybe Thatcher realized it was a setup, and he came after me because he believed I had betrayed him." Mercy, it made sense. "I knew there was a reason I didn't trust Parker."

"I could be wrong." Jack walked closer and looked down at her. "I can make some calls and find out what this deal with Thatcher was all about."

More calls. Added to the arrangements he'd have to make to keep them all safe. "I'm sorry I'm putting you through this."

He stood there, and a moment later he nodded. "I don't think this is your fault." He eased onto the edge of the sofa so that he was sitting next to where she was lying. "Your brother could be after your money. Parker could be trying to cover up something, and he could have inadvertently put Eldon Thatcher on your trail."

"And then there's Margaret and Ted. Maybe they're working for my brother. Or maybe not. I suppose it's possible they've been holding me all this time for their own monetary gain." Her gaze snapped to Jack's just as his jumped to hers. "My financial records. I need to go through them to see if someone's gotten into them."

He put his hand on her shoulder when she tried to get up. "I'd planned to do that after you were asleep."

Yet more work for him. "I can't rest. I need to help you."

"You can rest," he insisted. "Alana, I need you to have a clear head, and that won't happen until you sleep off the sedative Thatcher gave you."

She wanted badly to argue, but she wasn't sure she had the strength to put up a fight. "Can I at least take my nap in the room with Joey?"

"Trust me, you won't get a nap if you're in the room with him."

And at that moment, she heard her son giggle.

The right corner of Jack's mouth lifted. "See?" But the smile was soon replaced with a more serious expression. "Tell you what, I'll bring him in here for just a couple of seconds if you promise me you'll get some sleep."

"I promise." She had no choice. Sleep was going to come whether she wanted it or not. "It must be hard to be so nice to me."

She reached up to smooth away the worry lines on his forehead, but the moment she touched him, she knew it was a mistake. Even now, with all the danger and uncertainty, touching was out.

Jack snagged her hand to move it away. Or so she thought. But he held on to it, lacing their fingers together. He looked as if he were about to say something, but then he released the grip he had on her and started to stand.

Alana caught him. "What were you going to say?"

"Something stupid."

"Go ahead. Say it. With this fog in my head, I probably won't remember it anyway." And for some reason, that made her smile.

He locked gazes with her. "You can't take Joey from me."

Oh, she'd thought this was about the attraction, but she was wrong. Thankfully, one of them had his mind on the right track. And the right track was Joey.

Alana forced herself to come up with a possible solution, one that would get that dour expression off Jack's face. "What if I agree for us to split custody for now? Once Thatcher is caught, we can work out something more permanent."

The dour expression and the pain stayed. This was killing him. But it wasn't a walk in the park for her, either.

"Jack, I have to be a mother to my son." She paused. "But that doesn't mean I'll exclude you as his father. He calls you Da-Da, for heaven's sake. I can see the love you two feel for each other."

He didn't say anything for several moments. "Split custody," he repeated. He started to get up again.

Again, Alana stopped him. She wanted to tell him that she would be fair, that she wouldn't do anything intentional to hurt him or her son. Even if that meant she had to back off for a while.

"I don't get involved easily," he said, surprising her with this turn in the conversation.

"Neither do I." Her tone was cautious, and she waited for more.

"But there's this attraction." His tone was even more cautious than hers. "I'm guessing it's because of Joey?"

Maybe it was the hazy head, but she couldn't make the connection. "No. I don't think it has anything to do with him. You're a hot guy. It's simple attraction."

He seemed to give that some thought, and just when Alana was certain that he was indeed going to move away, she tightened her grip on his arm and dragged him down to her.

She kissed him.

Alana kept it brief. Hardly more than a peck. But her body reacted as if it were much more. The punch was like hot liquid fire. And she couldn't help but wonder what would happen if they really kissed.

He stayed close, his mouth hovering over hers. "This complicates the hell out of things, you know that?"

"I know. I should probably promise that it won't happen again."

"But it will," he disagreed.

"It will?" The only surprise was that he'd admitted it.

"Yeah. And if you figure out a way to stop it, let me know." He did stand then. "I'll bring Joey in."

Alana hated when he moved away from her. She lost his scent and his warmth all at once. Worse, she lost the sensation of his being there for her. She realized she'd gone a lifetime without feeling that.

Jack hadn't even made it to the door when there was a knock, and it opened. Reyes stuck his head into the room. "We got a problem, boss."

Alana groaned and sat up, bracing herself for the next round.

"A Texas Ranger just called," Reyes explained. He stepped inside, and Alana spotted the piece of paper he had in his hand. "When the Rangers got out to the Sauder Facility, the place was already on fire. They couldn't save anything. By the time the fire department arrived, the entire place was nothing but cinders and ash."

Jack cursed. So did Alana. This was a huge setback. There would almost certainly have been some kind of incriminating evidence in that house that might point to one or more of their suspects.

"There's more," Reyes said. "The mailbox didn't burn, and there was a note inside it. It was from our kidnapping suspect, Eldon Thatcher. The Ranger read it to me, and I wrote it down word for word."

Reyes looked at the paper he held in his hand. Then looked at her. "I'll give you the clean version. Thatcher says he's gonna kill you."

Alana had already suspected that, so she was more than a little surprised at her reaction. Maybe it was hearing the threat aloud that did it, but fear and worry dropped on her like a ton of bricks.

Jack took the note, read through it and then as if he'd declared war on it, he crumpled it into a ball.

"What did it say?" Alana asked, not at all certain that she wanted to know.

"Thatcher's a sick SOB," Reyes mumbled.

"What did it say?" Alana repeated.

"He thinks you sold him out to the FBI." Jack didn't look at her when he spoke. "He wants revenge. And he says he'll get it by taking Joey."

Chapter Ten

The sound of Joey's laughter cut through the silence in the hospital waiting room.

Joey grabbed on to a magazine-laded table and pulled himself to a standing position. He slapped at the surface as if to announce his victory. Joey had learned to pull himself up two days earlier, and he'd already mastered it. According to the baby books Jack had read, it wouldn't be long before Joey was walking.

Tessie applauded the feat, causing Joey to giggle again. From the other side of the room, Alana sat and watched. She was smiling, cataloging Joey's every move. She hadn't taken her eyes off him during their ten-minute wait for Dr. Bartolo to appear for her checkup.

Reyes was blocking the doorway that led to the corridor. Unlike Alana, his attention wasn't on Joey. Reyes was standing guard.

Jack had a dozen important things to do. Beefing up security at the ranch. Following up on the search for Eldon Thatcher. Helping Reyes process Thatcher's car and the crime scene in the hospital parking lot. Oh, yeah, and he had to keep his son and Alana safe.

That was primary in his mind.

And that was the reason both he and Reyes were at the hospital waiting. If the doc gave her a clean bill of health, the first thing Alana would want was to hold Joey. Jack wouldn't stop her.

But Alana wouldn't settle for just holding Joey. She'd want to be a major part of his life. And that meant Jack had something else to add to his to-do list. He had to consult his attorney. He had to do whatever it took to keep primary custody of Joey. Then he could control the situation and give Alana visitation rights.

Jack glanced in Alana's direction. She still had her attention fastened to Joey. That intense look told him everything. She might have offered to share custody with him, but she would probably change her mind.

First, though, she had to battle for her safety.

Jack heard footsteps in the corridor and eased his hand over the butt of his holstered gun. "It's the doc," Reyes let him know.

Reyes stepped inside, clearing the path for Dr. Bartolo to enter. The doctor glanced at Jack's posture. Then at Alana. "Go ahead into the examining room." He pointed to a door just a few yards away. "I need to run over to the lab and pick up your results."

Alana nodded and stood. Jack stood, too. He didn't intend to let Alana out of his sight. Reyes would do the same for Tessie and Joey.

"I see the worry in your eyes," Alana whispered as they went into the examining room.

Jack didn't deny it was there. He left the door open just a fraction so he could respond faster if there was an emergency.

"I had some time to think last night," she added.

He'd heard her tossing and turning. "You were supposed to be resting."

"I managed to do that, too." Her face said otherwise. Still, her chin lifted up, a gesture she probably hoped would make her appear resolved. It didn't work. She still looked tired. "All that thinking led me to a decision. I've decided to move to Willow Ridge."

Jack froze. "Move here?" He didn't like the sound of that. Not that he thought she would just disappear. But having her underfoot was not going to cool this attraction between them. And it would put her near Joey every single day. "We're back to talking about splitting custody?"

She shook her head. "No."

"No?" Jack forced himself to unfreeze, and walked closer so he could study her expression. She was tired, yes. But her eyes were suddenly a lot clearer than they had been.

"I decided you should keep custody for now."

Jack blinked. And replayed each word. After doing that several times, he was still certain he'd misunderstood. "Excuse me?"

She swallowed hard. "For the time being, I want you to have custody."

He'd heard her all right. It was exactly what he'd wanted to hear, but what he couldn't understand was why she was saying it. "Why the change of heart?"

"More like a reality check." She scrubbed her hands up and down her arms. "I don't need to remind you that my life's a mess. Someone wants me dead, and that's spilled over to Joey. I know you're doing your best to keep him safe. I heard you talking on the phone this morning. You're trying to increase security at the ranch."

He was. He'd even borrowed some ranch hands from neighbors and would have them patrol the pastures. "What does that have to do with custody?"

"Everything." She looked him straight in the eye. "I know you'll do what's necessary to protect Joey."

He would. But he didn't need full custody for that.

"I won't continue to be a burden to you," she added. Her words rushed out as if she'd rehearsed them. "Once we're at the ranch, I'll call and make arrangements for my own security. I can hire a P.I. Several of them. I want them searching for evidence to link Margaret and Ted or even my brother to what's going on. I can also press the Rangers to do more to find Eldon Thatcher. Then I can—"

Jack touched his fingers to her mouth. That simple reminder to slow down worked—she hushed and stared at him. "I can't let you do all the work, okay?" she continued. "Especially since I'm responsible for this."

Oh, man. He didn't want to go there. "Eldon Thatcher is responsible," he reminded her.

She shook her head, but her frustration and fear were evident. Jack knew those emotions well. He felt the same.

"I have this beautiful son," she muttered. Her voice was beyond shaky. "A son who's in danger, and everything I do still feels as if it's not enough. I should probably get out of town and put some distance between Joey and me, but I'm afraid if I leave, I won't be here to help protect him."

Again, he was right there on the same page with her. Nothing short of jailing Eldon Thatcher would be enough, and even that wouldn't solve all their problems.

"The fight's just started," Jack said. "It's a fight we'll win." Because the alternative wasn't an alternative at all.

And then he did something stupid.

He pulled her into his arms.

The embrace didn't seem so uncomfortable this time.

It felt natural.

What was it about Alana that made him want to get close? He didn't have time for sex. Heck, he didn't have time for a kiss. But that didn't stop him from brushing his lips over her forehead. Nor did it stop him from thinking about where all of this could go after everyone responsible had been caught.

"Let me deal with security," he told her. "Put everything else on hold for now."

She pulled back and stared at him. "I'm not as weak as I was yesterday or the night before when I staggered into your office."

"Yes." For some stupid reason, that nearly made him smile. "I can see that."

That strength would be trouble. As long as she was dazed and weak, he could pretend this closeness was all about protection. He could rationalize that she needed his shoulder. His arms. Heck, maybe she still did need them, but Jack was betting at the moment neither of them was feeling very protective.

She had a unique way of capturing his attention, and she did it by just being her.

Alana no longer wore his clothes. Reyes had brought

her one of his girlfriend's outfits. A snug denim skirt, lavender sleeveless top and flat sandals. The items probably weren't her usual fashion fare. After all, Alana came from money, and the outfit screamed *discount store*. But the clothes fit her like a glove.

A tight glove, that accentuated her every curve.

And suddenly those curves seemed as interesting and enticing as her mouth.

Oh, yes. She could definitely get his attention.

The door opened, and they jumped apart as if they'd been doing something wrong. Which wasn't far off the mark. Jack had been on the brink of kissing her blind.

"Everything okay?" Dr. Bartolo asked, noticing their contact and the reaction to being caught.

"You tell me," Alana countered. She cleared her throat, straightened her clothes and tried to look indignant. "What do my lab tests say?"

The doctor stayed quiet a moment. "That you're good to go."

Alana let out a gasp. Of relief, no doubt. Jack wasn't quite so relieved. "What about the virus?"

"No signs of it. The nurse took Alana's vitals when she checked in. No fever. Blood pressure and pulse were normal. It appears the virus was just a twenty-four-hour thing."

"I can hold Joey," she said, heading for the door.

Jack didn't stop her, but he did follow. So did Dr. Bartolo, but he only hung around a couple of seconds before he mumbled "good luck" and started for the corridor.

Tessie must have realized what was about to happen because she got to her feet. Joey was still batting the magazines on the table, and he turned, apparently aware that something major was going on.

Alana didn't make a mad run toward Joey. She slowed her steps and approached him with caution. She paused just a few seconds before she reached down and scooped him into her arms.

Joey looked at Jack for reassurance. After all, Alana was practically a stranger. But Joey didn't cry when she pulled him into a long embrace. His son babbled a little, but Alana's hair soon caught his attention. Joey tugged at one of the strands.

Jack looked around the room at everyone's reactions. Tessie had her hand pressed to her chest and was watching the embrace as if it were a train wreck. Alana's eyes were shiny with fresh tears. And Reyes was watching Jack. The deputy had his eyebrow cocked, questioning how Jack was taking all of this.

Jack didn't have a clue.

He didn't have to examine his feelings, either, because Reyes's cell phone rang. The man answered it, and Jack knew after just a couple of seconds that this call involved something major. He moved closer to Reyes in case they had to discuss business.

"That was Kirby," Reyes informed him. Kirby Ward, the night deputy who was manning the office. "He just got a visitor. Margaret Vargas."

The nurse from Sauder. Interesting. And surprising. "What does she want?"

"To talk to you and Alana. She told Kirby she needed to discuss the fire at Sauder."

Even more interesting. But Jack's first instinct was to refuse to have Alana present when he talked with the nurse. He didn't want to put her through that stress, and he wanted to get her settled into the ranch.

But maybe Margaret would say things to Alana that she wouldn't say to him. Better yet, it would get Alana away from Joey so that Jack could take a deep breath and figure out how he was going to deal with everything that'd happened.

"Go ahead and take Tessie and Joey to the ranch," Jack instructed Reyes. "Alana and I will meet with Margaret, see what she has to say."

Then he could finally get Alana to the ranch so he could get some work done. How, exactly, he didn't know, but he was thinking he might have to rotate Kirby, Reyes and himself at the ranch so they could get the evidence processed. Bodyguard duty was a necessity, but so was catching the man who'd tried to kidnap Alana. Added to all of that, he had to keep the town safe.

Tessie stepped forward to take Joey from Alana. His aunt did so hesitantly, and Alana was also hesitant about giving up the child. She kissed Joey's cheek and gave him a little wave. His son waved back, but not at Alana. At Jack.

Jack could almost feel Alana's heart breaking.

There wasn't time to dwell on it. Jack caught her arm to get her moving. The sooner they met with Margaret, the sooner he could do his job and get her to safety.

Tessie, Joey and Reyes were ahead of them in the corridor, but Jack had no trouble spotting Dr. Bartolo, and the man talking to the doctor.

Parker Howell.

"What's he doing here?" Alana mumbled.

But she didn't get an immediate answer to her question. The conversation abruptly ended, and Parker hurried off. Jack stopped in front of Dr. Bartolo, and they all watched as Parker exited through the front doors.

"Was Agent Howell looking for us?" Jack asked.

Dr. Bartolo shook his head. "Not exactly. He said he was in town to drop off some more flyers about a missing woman."

Right. Kinley Ford. Reyes had told him that the FBI and the Rangers wanted to find the woman, and he wished he could help. But he had enough to deal with.

"Parker also wanted to know Alana's medical condition," the doctor added. "He especially wanted to know if she was still experiencing memory loss. I told him I'd give the information to him if he got a court order."

Good. Jack didn't want to share anything with the man who seemed determined to take custody of Alana.

"This isn't the first time I've seen Agent Howell around here," the doctor added. "He's was at the hospital eight months ago, the night Alana disappeared."

Alana's eyes were wide when she looked at Jack. "Any reason you didn't mention this sooner?"

"I didn't remember it until I saw him today. All I recall was seeing him in the hall. I didn't make the connection to Alana until he asked about her just now."

"He saw me that night?" Alana clarified.

"Probably. Visitors weren't restricted."

That meant Parker might have been the last person to see Alana before she disappeared. Funny that the man hadn't come clean about his visit sooner.

That made Jack wonder. What else had Parker failed to mention?

With Alana in tow, Jack hurried toward the doors so

he could catch the agent and get some answers that Parker had obviously been dodging.

But Parker was nowhere in sight.

That made Jack even more suspicious. Even though he had a long list of things to do, he really needed to make the time to have a thorough chat with Parker. While he was at it, he needed to call an old friend in the FBI and make sure Parker was legit.

"I take it you don't remember anything about Parker's hospital visit eight months ago?" Jack asked.

"Nothing."

He was afraid of that.

Jack led her out the side exit where he'd left his SUV. Ahead of them, Reyes got Tessie and Joey into the cruiser and drove away in the direction of the ranch. Jack started for his office, which was four miles away in the opposite direction.

"I was obviously drugged that night," Alana continued. "I've been thinking about who and how that could have happened."

So had he. "You remember eating anything?"

"Just the food that Tessie brought me." But then she stopped. "Wait. I also had some orange juice. It was on the tray after I came out of the bathroom, so I had a few sips."

Orange juice could have masked the taste of a drug, and anyone could easily have placed the glass in her room. Her brother, Sean, was still Jack's prime suspect. Or maybe Eldon Thatcher had done it in an attempt to sedate Alana so he could get her quietly out of the hospital.

But how did Parker fit in?

It wouldn't be standard practice for an agent to drug

an informant, but that didn't mean he hadn't done exactly that. Maybe Parker thought the drug would make Alana comply with his plan. Then perhaps something had gone wrong? Maybe she'd wandered away before Parker could get to her?

"There are two issues here," Jack said, thinking out loud. "The diamond deal and your disappearance."

She turned in the seat, stared at him. "You think they're connected?"

"Not exactly. But Sean might have used the opportunity to capitalize. He might have rationalized that he was keeping you safe from Thatcher by locking you away at Sauder." Though that would have taken a mountain of rationalization. Still, when money was involved, Jack knew people could do all sorts of things.

"After our talk with Margaret, I want you to check your accounts and see if any money's missing," he instructed. "If it is, that might give me enough for a search warrant to go through your brother's financial records to see if he profited from your stay at Sauder."

Alana nodded. Then paused. "But does Parker fit into that?"

"Maybe. If Sean is the one who put you in Sauder, then maybe he drugged you so he could get you there. Or he could have worked with Parker to do that."

She made a face to indicate she wasn't sure she believed that. "You think Parker drugged me?"

"He was there at the hospital." Still, it was stretch. Unless…

Jack kept coming back to the possibility that Parker was dirty. And if he was truly was, then that made this situation even more complicated.

And dangerous.

"Don't borrow trouble," Alana mumbled. "Let's just focus on my brother and Thatcher for now. We can try to find a money trail leading to my brother while trying to capture Thatcher before he causes us any more problems."

Jack was about to agree when he heard a loud pop. Before the sound barely registered in his head, his SUV jerked to the right.

A blowout.

On the front passenger's-side tire. Alana's side.

He fought to keep the SUV on the road. But there was a second pop and another violent jerk of his vehicle. Jack knew he was losing control.

He also knew why.

Someone had shot out the tires.

He couldn't draw his weapon because he needed both hands on the wheel. He had to stay on the road. Because if he crashed, they would be sitting ducks.

"Do you see the shooter?" Jack asked.

"Shooter?" Judging from the way she blurted that out, she'd just realized what was happening.

His SUV careered off the asphalt and launched into the thick underbrush that flanked both sides of the road. He saw the sprawling live oak, but there was nothing he could do to stop. Still, he tried. He fought with the steering wheel, trying to wrench it in the opposite direction.

But it was too late.

"Hold on!" Jack yelled.

He barely got out the warning before his SUV slammed into the tree.

Chapter Eleven

The airbag punched into Alana, pinning her against the seat and smothering her. She couldn't move. Couldn't breathe. But she knew she had to do something.

Somewhere amid the trees and the wild shrubs, there was a gunman who was responsible for what had just happened.

And that man was probably Eldon Thatcher.

He'd shot out the tires, and that had caused Jack to lose control and career into the tree. Worse, this might be just the start of the attack.

Beside her, Jack batted aside his airbag. "Are you hurt?" he asked.

Alana quickly tried to take inventory of her body. Other than her constricted breathing, she wasn't in any real pain. But she was terrified.

Jack frantically drew his weapon from his shoulder holster. "Try to push down your airbag. I need to see if the shooter's coming."

Oh, God. Thatcher might be coming to finish them off.

With her heartbeat pounding in her ears, Alana

latched on to the airbag fabric and shoved it away so she could look out the windshield. Both it and her side window were shattered, making it impossible to see if they were about to be attacked.

"Get down!" Jack shouted.

It wasn't a moment too soon.

A bullet tore through the already shattered windshield and sent a spray of safety glass spewing right at them.

Jack cursed and took aim at the gaping hole that the bullet had left. He fired. The blast echoed through the cab of the SUV and caused Alana's ears to pound.

She thought of Joey. Her precious son. Alana prayed that this latest attack was confined only to Jack and her. Maybe Reyes had already gotten her baby to safety at the ranch. She didn't want Joey anywhere near this.

"Stay down. I need you to call nine-one-one." Jack's voice somehow made it over the noise in her own head, as he thrust his phone into her hand.

Before she could dial the first number, another bullet sliced through the metal roof. The large gash brought in heat and blinding sunlight. It was also a reminder of how little protection they had.

Even though her hands were shaking, Alana punched in the numbers, and Deputy Kirby Ward answered. "Someone's shooting at me and Jack," she practically shouted into the phone. And she gave the man their location as best she could.

Another shot fired.

Then another.

Both ripped through her side of the door and came so close that she could almost feel the heat from them.

She sank lower into the seat, but she knew that might not do her any good.

Jack levered himself up and returned fire.

"The deputy's on his way," she relayed to Jack. But the question was, would he get there in time? Or would his arrival just make him a target, as well?

"The guy's using a rifle," Jack let her know.

Because the adrenaline and her heartbeat were roaring through her, it took a moment for her to realize what that meant. The shooter was probably hiding behind some of that thick brush or even in a tree. He might not be close enough for Jack's gun to stop him.

The next bullet proved that.

It tore into the seat just above her head.

"Get on the floor!" Jack yelled.

She tried, though the airbag was in her way. Alana shouldered it aside and slid to the floor. For all the good it'd do. Those bullets were eating their way through the SUV, and there was no place safe she could hide.

"You need to get down, too," she told Jack. "You could be hit."

Just the thought of it made her sick. Jack was in this position because of her. She'd put him in danger, and he was taking the majority of the risk by trying to return fire.

Behind them, Alana heard the sound of a car approaching from the road. She didn't dare try to see who it was, but since there was no siren, it probably wasn't the deputy. It was likely an innocent bystander who could also be hurt by one of those flying bullets.

But just like that, the shots stopped.

The silence came so quickly that it caused yet another surge of adrenaline. She knelt there, waiting. Listening.

Jack glanced down at her. "The car must have scared off the shooter."

Good. Except that it meant the gunman might be getting away. Jack must have realized that, as well because he reached for the handle of his door.

Alana latched on to his arm. "You're not going out there."

"I have to."

She was about to argue that point, but she heard a welcome sound. A siren. Backup was close.

Jack pushed her hand from his arm and opened his door. Alana held her breath and prayed that the shots wouldn't start again.

They didn't.

There was only the sound of the siren and Jack's movements.

She levered herself up slightly, and through the hole in the windshield, she saw him take cover behind the tree. His gaze darted all around, looking for the person who'd just tried to kill them.

And then he looked down.

His attention snapped to her. "Get out of the SUV. The gas tank ruptured. If he shoots again, it could cause a fire."

"Oh, God." Alana didn't waste any time. She grabbed the handle, but when it wouldn't budge, she rammed her shoulder against the door to open it. Because of her position, she couldn't get her footing and tumbled onto the ground and scrambled for cover.

"Stay behind the tree," Jack instructed. "Get ready to run if he fires a shot at that gasoline." And then his attention snapped behind them.

For one terrifying moment, she thought maybe the

shooter had managed to sneak up on them, but Alana soon realized from the badge he wore that it was the deputy, Kirby Ward. He was young, probably not much older than twenty-one, with a slight build, but he was armed. The moment he was in place, guarding her, Jack stepped out from behind the tree.

Mercy, he was going out there. Alana wanted to tell him to stop, but she couldn't. The shooter was almost certainly Thatcher—a man who'd already tried to kidnap her—and he needed to be stopped. Still, this lull in the shots could be a ploy.

But Jack stepped out into the open anyway, just as another shot rang out.

Alana heard herself scream. She tried to move, to get to Jack so she could help him. But the deputy hooked his left arm around her and held on. She struggled, fighting him, but he wouldn't let go.

"I'm okay," Jack said. "The bullet didn't even come in this direction."

She stopped fighting and went limp with relief. Thatcher hadn't shot at Jack after all.

"What the hell?" Jack mumbled.

The deputy inched away from her and peered around the tree. Alana, too, wanted to know what had caused Jack's reaction.

Both Jack and Kirby had their attention fastened to something in front of the tree. They had their weapons aimed and ready, but neither looked on the verge of firing.

Jack cursed again and rushed out of her sight. Kirby did the same and shouted, "I'll call an ambulance."

An ambulance? Why? Had Thatcher shot himself?

She couldn't stay put. Alana eased out from the cover of the tree and spotted Jack and Kirby racing toward someone. A man. Staggering, he had a rifle in his hand, but he dropped it to the ground. And Alana soon realized why.

He wasn't surrendering, exactly. There was a bright red stain across the front of his shirt.

Blood.

He'd been shot in the chest.

It wasn't Eldon Thatcher.

It was Ted Moore, the security guard from Sauder.

Judging from Jack's and Kirby's reactions, they were just as surprised as she was.

Since the man was either dead or very close to it, Alana hurried out to the spot where Ted had fallen.

Jack crouched down, but Kirby kept watch around them in case the worst happened: another attack. But Ted certainly wasn't in any shape to continue shooting.

When she approached the man on the ground, Ted immediately angled his eyes in her direction. He opened his mouth and lifted his hand to point at her.

"I…" He drew in a labored breath. His hand dropped, but his gaze stayed fastened on her. "He took your money."

"Who?" Jack and Alana asked in unison.

Ted opened his mouth again, but he said nothing else. He sucked in one last thin breath and made a choking sound in his throat. And that was it.

Ted Moore was dead.

JACK TRIED TO MAKE HIMSELF APPEAR as calm as possible. Tessie looked terrified and her hands were shaking when she hugged him.

"You could have been killed," his aunt said under her breath.

Yeah. Alana, too. But they'd both made it out of the crash and the shooting without so much as a scratch. They'd gotten lucky. Unlike Ted Moore. And while Jack wasn't sorry about having a suspect out of the way, he would have preferred Ted alive. The man's death had left them with far more questions than answers.

Alana's hands were shaking, too, but that didn't stop her from picking up Joey the moment they walked into the family room of the ranch house. His son didn't look so apprehensive this time and offered Alana a tentative smile. When she smiled back, Joey began to babble.

Reyes walked to Jack's side. "I need to get out to the scene of the shooting. You can manage things here?"

"Yes." But the problem was, Jack didn't know what exactly he had to manage. Eldon Thatcher was still out there. Jack didn't know if Ted's death affected Thatcher or not. The men could have two entirely separate agendas, or they could have been partners.

"The medical examiner should have had time to check the body." Jack kept his voice low so that Tessie and Alana wouldn't hear. Thankfully, both women were engrossed in Joey's antics. "I need to know if that gunshot wound was self-inflicted."

"You think it was?"

Jack wanted to say yes. He wanted that to be true. But he had his doubts. It wasn't impossible to self-inflict with a rifle to the chest, but it wasn't the simplest of maneuvers. He settled for answering, "I'm not sure."

Reyes made a sound of agreement. "If Ted was murdered, that means someone else had to be out there."

Yeah. It did. And that's why Jack wouldn't be getting much sleep tonight.

"Check the area for any sign that Ted wasn't acting alone," Jack instructed. "I also want Margaret questioned. She insisted Alana and I meet her at the sheriff's office, so she might have known which route we'd be taking to get there. She might have set all of this up."

"It's possible. She left your office after Kirby responded to your nine-one-one for backup."

Not exactly a surprise, but it was a disturbing development. It could mean that all of them—Thatcher, Ted and Margaret—were working together.

If so, he had two more people to stop.

And then he had to figure out how Alana's brother, Sean, and Special Agent Parker Howell fit into all of this. He needed plenty of information, and he wasn't sure Alana was up to getting it. Still, he didn't have a choice. Yes, she was shaken from the shooting, but he had to do everything within his power to stop another attack.

Reyes made his exit, and Jack went to the front door to lock it and set the security alarm. All the doors and windows were wired, and while this wouldn't necessarily stop another shooting, it would alert him if anyone tried to break in.

Alana looked in his direction as Jack walked back into the family room. His expression must have said it all because she kissed Joey and handed him to Tessie. Jack could see the loss in her face. It was painful to hand over her son when she'd had so few precious moments with him. But there would be other moments.

Moments he'd have to learn to deal with.

"You need me to call about my financial records," Alana said. She blew out a deep breath and pushed her hair from her face.

Jack nodded, and that was Tessie's cue to head for the kitchen. "Joey's probably hungry by now. I'll fix you both something to eat, too." His aunt closed the double doors behind her.

He took your money, Ted had warned. It had to be checked. Alana definitely had more than enough money to make a greedy person do all sorts of criminal things.

Jack pointed to the laptop on a corner desk. "If you remember your account passwords, it might be faster."

She gave a choppy nod, went to the computer and got started right away. He watched her as she clicked her way to a bank Web site. Her hands were still shaking. She was probably close to an inevitable adrenaline crash. Even though this was critical, the task wouldn't stop the crash. Nothing would. Very soon, Alana would realize just how close she'd come to dying today.

"Someone changed the password," she let him know.

That didn't surprise him. A criminal would have done that as soon as he'd gotten control of the account, which wouldn't have been hard to do with Alana drugged. Heck, she might even have given the person the info.

Alana reached for the phone that was next to the laptop. "I'll call my assistant." But she stopped with her hand poised over the phone. "If I still have an assistant." She groaned and shook her head. "God knows what's happened to my business since I've been gone."

"Your brother said he managed it for you," Jack reminded her.

"That's what I'm afraid of." Anger flashed through her eyes, and she snatched up the phone. "I'm calling my assistant on her personal phone. I'm pretty sure I still remember the number."

Several moments later, Alana was speaking to her assistant, Deidre. Alana cut through the woman's questions about where she'd been and said, "I can't explain all of that now. Sorry." She paused. "Deidre, I need you to go through my accounts. All of them." Another pause. "Yes, I know it might take a while, but call me the second you know the balances."

The adrenaline had drained him, as well, so Jack pulled over a chair and sat down beside her. He listened to her responses, and judging from her expression, this conversation wasn't giving her much good news. When she finally hung up, worry had bunched up her forehead.

"Sean told my assistant that I was away on an extended vacation." The emotion caused her voice to break on the last word.

Jack had to tamp down some emotion, as well. But in his case, it was anger. "Wonder why he was so convinced you weren't in danger?" But Jack knew the answer to that. If Sean had been the one who'd kept her at Sauder—and it was looking more and more as if he was—he would have told her assistant that all was well so as not to raise any alarms. He wouldn't have wanted the police brought in.

But that made Jack wonder.

Why hadn't Agent Parker Howell done more to find her? He had to have suspected that Alana was in trouble. Sean might not have been aware of the diamond deal if he'd only been after control of her money, but Parker was certainly aware of it. Yet he hadn't been able to find her.

"I can't believe my brother might have done this to me," Alana said. She stood and shook her head. She squeezed her eyes shut.

Jack stood, too, aware that they were too close. Practically toe-to-toe.

She leaned her head against him, her body brushing against his, but then she immediately jerked back.

"Sorry," she mumbled.

So was he. Sorry that she'd backed away. Despite being on the verge of a meltdown, Alana had remembered the dangerous attraction between them. But Jack was suddenly having a hard time following her lead.

Alana looked up at him. And the restraint she'd shown just moments earlier went south.

It happened fast. She leapt to her toes. He swooped down on her. Their mouths met. Man, did they ever! This was no gentle sweet kiss to offer comfort. This was hot and hungry.

Jack grabbed her. Like his kiss, this was no soft embrace. He snapped her to him. Alana didn't resist. She went willingly and upped the stakes by coiling her arms around his neck. That put their bodies directly against each other.

But he knew he was playing with fire.

He just didn't care.

He wanted this heat. He wanted Alana. Even if wanting her didn't make sense. Soon, very soon, they'd battle for custody of Joey, and the memory of this kiss wouldn't help. But did that make him stop?

No.

Jack only pulled her closer. He slid his hand around the back of her neck and deepened the kiss. That caused the fire inside her to burn even hotter. Her breasts pressed against his chest. Their mouths moved in some frenetic dance to find pleasure.

Her sex brushed against his. There it was. That punch. The reminder of where a good kiss usually led. To sex. In the back of his mind, he knew he couldn't go there, but that didn't stop him, either.

Alana voiced a throaty moan of pleasure and shifted her position, moving against him, her body against his erection. She wanted more of that contact, and she shoved him against the wall. It wasn't gentle. He landed with a thud.

Alana landed against him.

Exactly where he wanted her to be.

Jack trailed the kisses to her neck. It tasted just as good as her mouth and revved his body up another notch. Alana took things even further when her hand trailed down his side and then to his stomach. When her hand started to go even lower, Jack knew he had to do something or he'd end up having sex with her right then, right there.

He spun her around so that it was her back against the wall, and caught her hands, pinning them, so that she couldn't do any more of that mind-blowing touching. He kissed her one last time, and forced himself to pull back.

Their eyes met. He'd hoped to see some sane, rational regret in the depths of all that blue, but all he saw was the heat no doubt mirrored in his.

"Wow," she said. Somehow, that said it all.

He'd expected a kiss with Alana to be good, but he hadn't expected the out-of-control crazy stuff reserved for lust-crazed teenagers.

"We can't have sex, can we?" she asked.

It was a question his body wanted to answer, *Yes, we can.* But he ignored his body and tried to sound like a responsible adult. "Just an hour ago, we were under attack. This is a reaction to that."

She stared at him. Her eyes narrowed slightly. That was the only warning he got before she lunged forward. Even though he had her hands still pinned, her mouth landed right on his. No restraint. Nothing held back.

Alana kissed him.

What little composure he'd garnered just washed away, and when she finally pulled back, he knew this wasn't a reaction to the shooting. It was a human reaction. Pure basic primal attraction. He wanted her naked. He wanted to be inside her. He didn't care if it was wrong or if it complicated the hell out of things.

They stood there staring at each other, their breaths hot and fast. Not moving. He didn't dare move. Because if Alana brushed against his erection one more time, he'd lose control.

"We can't kiss again," she said.

"I don't want this to get mixed up with what's going on with Joey." Jack wanted it out there in the open.

"Trust me. This had nothing to do with the love I feel for my son."

Jack could have said the same thing. But was it true? Had parenthood forged some kind of strange bond between them?

He looked at her again. At her hair that he'd mussed when he grabbed her. At her kiss-reddened lips. At the flush of arousal still on her face.

Nope.

This wasn't about parenthood. And that meant it was a massive problem. Sex with Alana now seemed inevitable. Instead of facing each other as adversaries on the custody issue, they'd face each other as lovers.

That might make them more amicable to a settlement, but it might also cost him full custody of Joey. Because he'd have feelings for her. He'd be sympathetic. He might not fight as hard, and he needed to fight to keep his son.

The phone rang, the sound slicing through the room, and delivering yet another dose of much-needed reality. It was a reminder that he was in the middle of the most important case of his career.

Though she was obviously still shaken from the kiss, Alana reached behind her, located the phone and answered it. "Deidre," she said. "What did you find?"

Jack moved away from Alana to give them both some breathing room. He wanted her full concentration on the call and the crucial information she was getting from her assistant. While she was doing that, Jack composed himself. What he needed was a cold shower. That might cool him down and bring him back to his senses.

"I see," Alana commented. "And what about the other investment and business accounts?"

Judging from Alana's suddenly slack jaw, this wasn't good news. Jack had expected that. Hopefully, though, it was news that would help them find out what was really going on.

He walked to the window and checked the grounds.

There was a ranch hand out front. The man was armed and standing guard. They wouldn't get much ranching done, but he needed the security to keep Alana, Tessie and Joey safe.

When Alana ended the call, Jack turned back around to face her. She'd gone pale. "My half of the profits of the jewelry business hasn't been touched in eight months except to cover normal operating expenses. But my trust fund has been drained, and there's little money left in any of my investment accounts."

"How much is missing?"

"Over three million dollars."

Jack cursed. He'd just found a motive for why someone had wanted Alana locked away.

Alana sank onto the chair and blew out a long, weary breath. "Thankfully, the business account is still there. It's worth nearly twice that amount."

"This is the business you share with Sean?"

She nodded. Her eyes questioned their theory about her brother being behind this. If this was solely about money, why hadn't Sean gone after her business account? That would have been easier than tapping into her trust and investments.

Maybe he hadn't touched the business money because he needed that in place for his own business ventures.

"Deidre said she has my personal laptop. She took it from the office and brought it home with her," Alana continued. "She was afraid without anyone around, someone might steal it. She said she's opening the files now to see if she can find anything about the missing money. If there is, she'll call me right back."

It was a long shot. Truth was, the money probably

hadn't started to disappear until after she was at Sauder, or Alana would have noticed the missing funds.

Jack was about to pull her into his arms for a hug of comfort, but his cell phone rang. He checked the screen and saw that it was Reyes. This could be yet another important call.

"I just talked with the M.E.," Reyes explained. "He got out here about a half hour ago and has been examining Ted Moore's body."

"And?"

"He says there's no evidence of close-range residue around the wound. No stippling, either. The entrance wound is about .50-caliber size."

Jack groaned. That meant the gun hadn't been close enough to Ted's skin to leave any soot or residue from the unburned gunpowder. The caliber size was an indication that the shot had come from a long-range rifle. A sniper rifle, it was sometimes called.

Ted hadn't killed himself.

A bullet of that size would have made a much larger hole if Ted had shot himself at point-blank range. So the shooter was some distance away.

"There's more," Reyes continued. "I just checked out Ted's rifle, and I don't even think it's been recently fired. I'll bring it in for testing."

"Good. Collect any bullet fragments from my SUV," Jack instructed, knowing that Reyes already had that on his to-do list. "Also, look for shell casings. I'll be here at the ranch if you need me."

"Bad news?" Alana asked the moment he hung up.

Jack nodded. "No suicide. Thatcher must have murdered Ted with an assault rifle."

Alana shook her head. "But Ted had a rifle, too."

"He had a .22, and Reyes didn't think it'd been fired." Jack had noticed that when the man first staggered out of the woods.

She stayed quiet a moment. "Then what was Ted doing out there?"

He shrugged. "We probably won't know the answer to that until I talk to Thatcher."

Something he couldn't do until the man was captured. Jack didn't doubt that would happen. Thatcher would likely make another attempt to kill them. And Jack would do whatever was necessary to protect Alana and Joey. This wouldn't end until he put a bullet in Thatcher. He only hoped he would get answers first—he didn't want Alana to go through her life wondering why she'd been put through hell and back for the past eight months.

The house phone rang, and when Jack went to answer it, he saw on the caller ID that it was from Alana's assistant, Deidre. He picked up the phone and handed it to Alana.

She looked unsteady. Probably from the news he'd just delivered. But maybe this call would give them something positive.

"December twenty-fourth," Alana mumbled. "I don't remember going to work, but there are a lot of things I don't remember. What did the letter say exactly?" She paused. "Who was to get this letter?" She mumbled something, as if trying to jog her memory. "There was no address information at all?"

Jack heard the woman answer "no."

"Okay. Maybe that's in another note somewhere. What did I write in this letter?" Alana asked.

Jack saw Alana's eyes widen. She drew in a sharp breath and dropped back a step.

"Deidre, could you please repeat that? I want to write it down to make sure I didn't misunderstand." Alana's hands were far from steady when she grabbed the pen and paper next to the phone.

Jack leaned in so he could see what she wrote.

"Special Agent Parker Howell withheld information about the diamond deal he's investigating. He informed me that the buyer is a man named Eldon Thatcher, but after contacting colleagues, I've learned Mr. Thatcher is only one of two interested buyers."

Buyer, not seller. What was going on?

"The other potential buyer is from Willow Ridge." Alana wrote what her assistant was reading to her. "And I intend to contact him."

Jack held his breath and watched as Alana jotted down the name of the person who was ultimately connected to all of this.

"Dr. Keith Bartolo."

Chapter Twelve

Her life might be far from perfect, but her son certainly was.

Alana tried to read Joey one of the books from a stack in his room but finally gave up. He was far more interested in trying to wrestle with a large stuffed teddy bear. The bear was bright blue, the color of Joey's shirt and shorts, and was twice his size.

Joey giggled when he and the bear toppled onto the thickly carpeted floor.

Alana giggled, too.

Tessie and Jack looked as if they'd just heard a foreign sound. That wasn't far from the truth. It'd been months since she'd laughed, and it might be a while before she did it again. This precious time with her son was a too-brief interlude.

Soon, Joey would be leaving.

The packed bags in the hallway were proof of that. Any minute now, a sheriff friend of Jack's would arrive to whisk Tessie and Joey away. Part of Alana wanted to be whisked away with them. She wanted to get as far from the danger as possible, but going with her son would ultimately put him right back in the line of fire. He'd be safer away from her.

And her heart would break.

She'd already lost so much time with him. She didn't want to lose a moment more. But maybe, just maybe, Jack's deputies and the Texas Rangers could find Thatcher quickly so that her time away from Joey would be very short indeed.

Joey giggled again, and crawling, he tried to drag the bear to Jack, who was in the doorway. Like Alana, he'd changed clothes since the shooting and now wore another pair of those great-fitting jeans and a black shirt. There was no evidence of the struggle on these clothes. No grass stains, no powdery debris from the airbag, no smell of gunshot residue. That didn't mean, however, she couldn't see and smell those things.

It would be a long while before that particular nightmare faded, and judging from the stark emotion in Jack's eyes, he felt the same.

Jack had spent hours making the arrangements for Joey's safety, all while also trying to contact Dr. Bartolo.

But Dr. Bartolo wasn't answering his phone, and his nurse said she didn't know where he was. That didn't make him look innocent, and Alana had to admit that Bartolo might have had something to do with her disappearance. But then, she hadn't trusted him and had gotten the willies when he strolled into Jack's office the night of her arrival.

The doorbell rang, and Alana's heart clenched. It was probably the sheriff coming for Joey, but she automatically scooped her son into her arms and moved to the far side of the room, just in case she had to protect him. Jack nodded, turned and went to answer the door.

Joey didn't fuss about Alana's tight grip. Perhaps he sensed something was wrong. He stared at her with suddenly intense eyes. Joey had gotten his eye color from her, but his expression was all Jack. Jack might not have been Joey's biological father, but she could see so much of him in the little boy.

Jack opened the door and she heard voices. *Friendly* voices. Which meant this wasn't the threat her body had prepared itself for. It was a threat of a different kind. Alana kissed Joey's cheek and said a quick prayer that he would soon be returned safely to her.

"What's gonna happen?" Tessie asked.

Alana didn't think the woman's question was about the little trip Joey and she were about to take. "I don't know," she answered honestly.

"Jack loves that little boy, you know."

"I know. I love him, too."

Tessie walked closer, smiled at Joey and gently rubbed his back. "And how do you feel about Jack?"

Alana opened her mouth. Then she closed it, hoping an acceptable answer would come to mind. It didn't. She was thankful for Jack. But there was also an attraction between them that had reached the boiling point. Worse, it was probably clouding her feelings for him. She was starting to dream of them being a family.

Thinking of Jack as a lover, as her protector and Joey's father, made a great package. One she should resist. Because if she did become his lover, she didn't want these other things playing into the equation. Sex for her meant making love. It meant a commitment, and neither Jack nor she was ready to go there.

Alana heard footsteps, and a moment later, a lanky brown-haired man appeared in the doorway with Jack.

"This is Sheriff Beck Tanner from LaMesa Springs," Jack said, making the introductions.

He looked capable and trustworthy enough, but Alana wished that Jack could be the one to protect Joey. Love was a huge motivator, and she knew Jack would put his life on the line for her little boy. Still, Jack couldn't be in two places at once, and he had to be in Willow Ridge to catch Thatcher.

Tessie reached for Joey, and Alana gave him one last kiss before the woman took him. There was no way she could stop her tears. Alana was more than a little surprised to see tears in Tessie's eyes, too.

"I'll take care of him. I promise," Tessie whispered. "You take care of Jack, okay?"

In that moment Alana no longer felt at odds with the woman, and she pulled both Tessie and Joey into a quick hug. "I will," she whispered back.

Tessie eased away, and Jack kissed Joey goodbye. There were no tears in Jack's eyes. Just the look of a man determined to succeed.

"You've got the trip mapped out?" Jack asked Sheriff Tanner. He picked up the suitcases, one in each hand, and headed for the door.

"All loaded in the GPS," Sheriff Tanner assured him. "I'm not taking a direct route. And I'll make sure no one follows. My deputy is also with me, just in case. I'll call you the minute we get to the house."

"Thanks," Jack said. Alana echoed the same.

Sheriff Tanner opened the door, and Alana saw his white SUV parked outside. The windows had a dark tint, but with the slant of the late afternoon sun, she could see the outline of a man in the backseat. Tanner's deputy, no doubt.

"Wait inside," Jack instructed.

Alana did and watched as the others hurried to the vehicle. Within just a few seconds, Jack had the suitcases loaded, Tessie put Joey in the child-restraint seat, got inside the vehicle and the sheriff drove away.

It felt as if someone had stomped on her heart.

Jack hurried back up the steps and caught her arm to pull her back inside. He shut the door and locked it.

"Try not to dwell on it," he mumbled.

An impossible task, but he was right. She didn't need to think about her son's departure.

Or the fact that she and Jack were now alone in the ranch house.

There was only one thing that would speed up her son's return and that was capturing the person who wanted her dead. To do that, she had to learn the truth.

Jack immediately got to work. He took out his cell phone, called Reyes and asked for an update on Dr. Bartolo while he went into the family room and turned on the laptop. Alana didn't waste time, either. She looked at the notes she'd made earlier during her phone call with her assistant. The last thing she'd written was Dr. Bartolo's name. The man could be a key to this investigation.

"Dr. Bartolo still isn't answering any of his phones," Jack let her know. He sat down at the computer. "No one's seen him in the past two hours."

Bartolo could have disappeared. Maybe he learned

Jack and she were on to him. But how would he have known that? Earlier that morning, he hadn't shown any signs of concern during her checkup. Of course, the doctor could also be in danger. If the culprit behind all of this wanted to make sure Jack and she didn't speak to Bartolo, the doctor could have been kidnapped.

Or worse.

That made the situation even more urgent. If Bartolo was in grave danger, in addition to finding him, they needed to figure out how he played into the investigation. And why Parker had lied and said Thatcher was selling instead of buying those illegal diamonds. Had the man just made an honest mistake, or was it more sinister than that?

Alana glanced at her notes again. "Who was this letter to?"

"Maybe you were going to send it to Parker's boss?" Jack turned, looked up at her. "Maybe to me."

That made sense. "I might have wanted you involved if I suspected Dr. Bartolo." And something else made sense. "This could explain why I was in Willow Ridge eight months ago. I probably came to see you about the doctor. Since I was pregnant, I doubt I would have gone to see him on my own."

He nodded, and scratched his head. "You still don't remember any of this?"

"Bits and pieces. For instance, I remember sitting at my desk and typing that letter, but I don't know why I changed my mind about sending it. I don't know why I decided to come here in person instead of just calling you."

"Maybe because you thought someone might listen in on your conversation."

"Sean," she mumbled. "Or maybe I thought Parker, Thatcher or even Dr. Bartolo had bugged my office." Alana paused and let that sink in. She drifted back to that day and remembered her feelings. Fear. She'd definitely known she was in danger.

And yes, she'd been on her way to talk to Jack.

Though instead of meeting him at his office, she'd realized someone was following her. Just like that, fear rippled through her. "A dark blue van followed me from San Antonio. I remember it."

Jack stood and ducked down a little so they'd be eye to eye. He caught her shoulders. "Keep going. What else do you recall?"

"The van bumped into my car." Her heart started to race, just as it had that day. "I sped up, but there was ice on the road. I skidded, and the van managed to get around me and drive off."

"Probably because the driver saw me coming," Jack provided.

Yes. That made sense. The images were no longer fuzzy and clipped. They came at her like gunshots. "I lost control and crashed through the bridge railing."

She felt the jolt of the impact all over again. The freezing water that gushed into her car. Panicking, she'd fought, first with the airbag and then the seat belt. "I got free, but I couldn't get out of the car. The door was jammed."

"It's okay." Jack's voice sounded miles away. So did his touch, even though Alana was aware that he'd pulled her into his arms. "It's okay," he repeated.

He was trying to calm her down. With reason. Alana thought she might be on the verge of a panic attack. She couldn't catch her breath, and everything was starting to race out of control, just as it had when she was in that water.

"Think back to the van," Jack instructed, his voice level and reassuring. "I didn't see it, but I wasn't exactly looking for it when I spotted your car go off that bridge. Did you see the license plates or get a glimpse of the driver?"

Had she? Though it wasn't easy, Alana pushed aside her emotions and concentrated. She tried to replay everything that had happened from the moment she realized the van was following her. "I couldn't see the driver, but I saw the front bumper. It had Texas plates."

"Good. You remember any of the numbers or letters?"

She shook her head. "No. But it was a rental. I remember seeing a decal for State Rental. Does that help?"

"You bet. I'll make some calls and see if they have a record of someone renting a dark blue van eight months ago. We might get lucky."

Finally. A break.

He went to the computer, clicked his way to an official-looking site and typed in some information about the incident and the rental car. "I'm requesting assistance from the San Antonio P.D. State Rental is headquartered there. They'll send an officer over to check the records."

Alana blew out a long breath and prayed for the best, even if it led her in the direction of her brother. Right now the truth was the only thing that would bring her little boy back home.

Jack stood again, but instead of moving closer to her, he crammed his hands in his pockets. "What did Tessie whisper to you before she left?"

"Oh." Alana scratched her head, not because she didn't remember, but because it took her a moment to switch from the case to more personal matters. "She wanted me to promise to take care of you. I said I would."

The corner of his mouth lifted, and a dimple flashed in his right cheek. The smile quickly faded, though. "If we get into another situation like we did today, I want you to take cover. I want you behind me."

She didn't want to think of another situation like that occurring. Alana was still too raw from the memories she'd just had to relive. "Behind you?" she questioned, tongue-in-cheek. "You're sure that'd be any safer?" She made sure she punctuated the question with a smile.

His smile didn't return, but he eased his hand from his pocket, reached out and skimmed his fingers over her cheek. He sent little sparks over her entire body. "I'm the sheriff. It's my job to protect you."

There went the sparks and what was left of her smile.

"No," he said quickly. "I didn't mean it like that." He pulled back his hand, shook his head and cursed. "I didn't mean it like that, either."

Because she totally understood his confused state of mind and because she wanted to feel those sparks again, she came up on her toes and kissed him. Not hot and French, the way she wanted. Alana pressed her mouth to his cheek, right at the corner of his lips. It was an invitation. And then she waited to see what Jack would do next.

He stood there. "If I kiss you, we'll have sex," he announced.

"Oh." She felt a primal tug deep within her belly and

tried to look shocked. She wasn't, though. She knew what Jack wanted. What she wanted.

They wanted each other.

They stared at each other, both waiting for the other to back away. But it didn't happen, because Jack's cell phone rang.

Until that ring, Alana hadn't realized just how ready she was to be dragged off to bed. Yes, the timing was terrible, but she wanted Jack more than she'd ever wanted another man. Still, she would have to wait.

Jack snatched the phone from his pocket and glanced at the screen. "It's one of the ranch hands."

A call could mean he'd spotted someone suspicious. Like Thatcher.

Jack hurried across the room and looked out the window. Alana followed, her heart now in her throat. God, how could her emotions rifle so quickly from passion to out-and-out fear?

"What does he want?" Jack asked.

Alana looked over his shoulder and spotted the dark blue car stopped just on the other side of a cattle gate. There stood the ranch hand on the phone. He'd apparently prevented the car from getting any closer to the house.

"All right," Jack said a moment later. "Let him in." He hung up, slipped the phone back into his pocket and drew his gun from his shoulder holster.

"Who's out there?"

"Special Agent Parker Howell, Margaret Vargas and your brother. Parker says he wants to talk, that he knows who's behind the plot to kill you."

Chapter Thirteen

Jack kept Alana behind him and his gun ready when he opened the door.

Yes, Parker was a federal agent, but Jack didn't trust the man any more than he did the pair that Parker had brought with him. But Jack didn't want that to get in the way of Alana and him learning the truth.

Parker froze when he spotted the gun and his left eyebrow shot up. "Is that necessary?"

"Yeah, it is," Jack snapped.

Three suspects were on his porch, and he wasn't about to let down his guard. In fact, he had no plans to let them in, period. Parker stepped forward, but Jack blocked his path.

Parker huffed. So did Sean, while staring at his sister. But Margaret was looking around as if she expected someone to gun her down at any moment. Since that might not be too far from the truth, Jack decided to get to the point.

"You said you knew who was trying to kill Alana," he said to Parker.

"Yes." Parker looked around, as well. "But I don't

think it's wise to discuss it out here. I have proof that Eldon Thatcher is in the area. A credible eyewitness put him at a convenience store just outside Willow Ridge."

Jack didn't doubt it. In fact, he believed Thatcher had fired those shots earlier and had probably murdered Ted. The trick now was to find out not only where Thatcher was but how this trio of visitors fit into what was happening.

"I think Thatcher's trying to kill me, too," Margaret volunteered. "That's why I asked Parker to put me in protective custody. I think Thatcher will come after me because he might believe I can connect him to the Sauder Facility. I saw him near the place not long after Alana escaped." Margaret looked nervous, but Jack wasn't completely buying it. She could be faking to throw suspicion off her.

"Did you set us up?" Jack asked her when she didn't continue. "Because I think it's more than suspicious that Alana and I were nearly killed on the way to meet you."

The woman frantically shook her head. "I didn't have any part in that. I just wanted to meet with you. To talk. And to ask for protection."

"She's terrified for her life," Parker added. "Now, can we come in?"

Jack didn't have to think about this one. "No."

"No?" Sean challenged. He shoved his way around Parker but stopped when Jack put the gun in his face.

"No," Jack repeated. He didn't lower the gun until Sean stepped back. "Here's how this'll work. You three will give me answers and then leave. I don't want you near Alana any longer than necessary."

"I'm your brother." Sean aimed his narrowed eyes at his sister.

"Yes," she agreed. She maneuvered herself to Jack's side so she was facing Sean. "But I don't trust you. Someone stole a lot of money from me while I was drugged and locked away at that so-called institution."

"Well, it wasn't me," Sean insisted.

"Nor me." Margaret was adamant about it. "I didn't know you were sane when you there. The commitment letter said you were delusional and violent."

"And you didn't see anything to indicate otherwise?" Jack asked.

Margaret dodged his gaze. "Sometimes, when Alana was heavily drugged, Ted would have her sign papers. I asked him what that was all about, but he said it was just routine, that the owner of the institution required it. I thought that was odd. I mean, Ted was just a guard. Plus, if she was truly insane, then her signature wouldn't have held up in court or anything."

Alana folded her arms over her chest. "Why didn't you get me out of there? Or at least question what was going on? Instead, you turned a blind eye and collected a paycheck."

"And now I might have to pay for that with my life." Margaret swallowed hard, turned and headed back toward the car. "I'm not standing out here in the open any longer. Thatcher is nearby," she whispered, her voice a terrified warning. "Can't you feel him?"

Jack didn't have the woman's same eerie premonition, but the lawman in him made him take a look around. There was no sign of Thatcher, but he didn't like the idea of this outdoor meeting going on much longer.

"We'll follow the money trail," Jack told Parker. "It's not easy to hide a sum that large and not set off alarms." He aimed an accusing glare at Sean.

Parker nodded. "The FBI's already investigating it. In fact, we've learned something that will lead to an imminent arrest. I plan to make that arrest as soon as I leave here. I just wanted to come out and speak to Alana first, so I could update her on the case."

"And the person you'll be arresting?" Jack asked.

"Dr. Keith Bartolo." Parker seemed very confident about his answer. "I can't get into specific details yet, but the FBI believes he's the one who's trying to kill Alana."

Jack and Alana exchanged glances. "How does Thatcher fit into this?" Alana wanted to know.

"At first I thought Thatcher might be operating alone, but now I think he might be working for Dr. Bartolo. That's what the financial records seem to indicate, anyway. Someone is definitely paying Thatcher, and the money seems to be coming from an offshore account set up by Dr. Bartolo."

Hell. If it was true, then Alana's attacker had had hands-on access to her. Bartolo had even been alone with her.

Alana folded her arms over her chest. "Why exactly would Dr. Bartolo want me dead?"

Parker shrugged as if the answer was obvious. "Because he didn't want to go to prison for an illegal diamond deal. When the deal backfired, I think he drugged you and took you to Sauder. And I think he set up the institution so he could milk your accounts and keep you from going to the authorities."

"I think Bartolo took out the money slowly, over several months, so I wouldn't get suspicious," Sean piped in. "If he'd emptied the accounts all at once, the bank would almost certainly have contacted me."

True. But Jack still wasn't sure all of this added up. It was possible that the answer was very simple, that Thatcher had acted alone. That Thatcher had drugged Alana and put her in Sauder and that it was Thatcher alone who wanted her and Margaret dead so all loose ends would be tied up. With Ted dead, he'd have no witnesses to his crime. Thatcher could even have set up Bartolo to take the blame.

But Jack didn't want to risk Alana's life on a theory.

Any of the three in front of him could have put this plan together. Three million dollars was a huge motive to hold a woman against her will and commit murder.

"Earlier you said Eldon Thatcher was trying to sell illegal diamonds," Jack tossed out to Parker. And he waited.

Parker didn't react to that. "He tried. Why do you ask?"

"Because I heard some contradictory information."

"Really?" There was a flicker of emotion in his eyes. "I'd be interested in the source of that information."

"I'll get back to you on that," Jack countered. But it wouldn't happen soon. Not until he was sure Parker was clean and Alana was safe.

Parker reached out to Alana, but then withdrew his hand when she recoiled. "Alana, I want you in the FBI's protective custody, at least until after Bartolo and Thatcher have been arrested."

She shook her head. "I'm staying here."

"Don't you see what you're doing?" Sean cursed. "You trust this local yokel because you've let your heart get in the way of making a sound logical decision. Or maybe you think cozying up to him is the fastest way to get your son back?"

Alana stepped closer and met her brother eye-to-eye. "I trust Jack."

"Really? And what about your life? Your business? Your future? You trust him with that, too?"

"Yes." She spoke so firmly that Jack looked at her to see her expression. It was firm, too. This was no longer the frightened woman who'd staggered into his office.

Sean cursed again. "You're making another mistake."

And then he did something that surprised Jack. Sean reached out and tried to hug his sister. However, Alana jerked away from him. "The biggest mistake I could make would be to allow you to worm your way back into my life."

"I'm your brother," he reminded her again.

"We share common DNA, but you don't know the meaning of the word *brother*. Rather than inconvenience yourself, you turned your back on my son. He nearly became a ward of the state because of you. And the whole time I was in Sauder, you didn't even try to find me."

"I did try. And you're not thinking straight. Alana, you're not yourself."

"You're wrong. I am myself, and I know what I want. I want you out of my life." She turned and went back into the house.

Good. She was out of the line of fire, both literally and where her brother was concerned. Alana had some bad blood with Sean, and Jack didn't want her to have to deal with that on top of everything else. Still, it'd probably done her some good to stand up to him.

"You're sure about keeping Alana here?" Parker asked.

Sean didn't wait for the answer. He stormed back to the car.

"I'm sure. Besides, she shouldn't have to be in protective custody too long if you're right about Dr. Bartolo and you can arrest him."

"Oh, I'm right."

"You know where he is?" Jack didn't let the conversation distract him. He glanced around the yard to make sure Thatcher wasn't there.

"Not exactly. But I have someone out looking for him. He's not answering his phone, and he's not in his office. Any idea where he could be?"

"None. In fact, I'm anxious to speak to him myself."

"Yes, I'll bet you are." Parker glanced around, as well. "A word of advice, Jack. This is an FBI investigation now, and I don't want you to get in the way."

Jack tried not to let that rile him, but it did. "I'll get in the way as long as Alana's in danger."

"You're personally involved with her," Parker concluded. "That could be a fatal mistake."

Jack couldn't argue. But he also couldn't go back and undo those kisses that he and Alana had shared. He could only be vigilant and pray that was enough. Because the stakes were way too high for him to fail.

Jack shut the door, locked it and reset the security system. He looked out the sidelight window to make sure their visitors weren't hanging around. When the car finally pulled away, he took out his phone.

"Who are you calling?" Alana asked. She went to the window and watched Parker and the others drive away.

"I'm trying Dr. Bartolo's number again."

Her eyes widened. "You're not going to warn him that he's about to be arrested?"

"No. But I want his side of the story before Parker gets to him."

He scrolled through the cell phone list, located the number and pressed Dial. He waited. One ring. Two. Three.

Someone picked up on the fourth. But whoever it was didn't say anything. But Jack could hear breathing. "Dr. Bartolo?" he greeted.

The seconds dragged by. "Yes."

Jack let out the breath he'd been holding. "Where are you? I've been looking for you."

"I know. I got the messages you left on my voice mail. Jack, I'm in trouble."

It was a Texas-size understatement, but Jack kept that to himself. "What do you mean?"

"I think someone's trying to kill me."

"Welcome to the club." Inside, Jack wasn't so cavalier, and he was more than curious. "Who wants you dead?"

More silence. "Last year I got involved with the wrong people. I heard about some diamonds for sale, and I thought they'd be a good investment. The price was right. The deal wasn't."

"Go on," Jack said when the man stopped. He held the phone closer so that Alana could hear.

"I didn't know the deal involved illegal diamonds. I swear, I didn't know." The doctor sounded convincing. But was he telling the truth?

"How did you find out about these diamonds?"

The doctor hesitated again. "Sean Davis."

Well, Jack had expected that name to pop up. "Alana's brother?"

"Yes. I met him through friends, and he told me about a collection of diamonds that he could get for me at rock-bottom cost. He wanted to go halves with me, with both of us putting up the cash."

Jack looked at Alana. She'd gone pale. "Did you have anything to do with Alana's disappearance?"

"No." But he no longer sounded convincing. "I didn't even know who she was until after she'd disappeared. Davis is a common name. When she came to the hospital in labor, I didn't make the connection. And I didn't know the diamond deal was illegal until the FBI contacted me days after her disappearance."

Jack wasn't sure he believed that, either.

"I think Sean wants me dead now," the doctor continued. "I think I'm the only one who can link him to the diamond deal."

"That seems like an extreme reason to murder someone." But it wasn't, especially if the diamonds were also connected to Alana's being held prisoner and having her trust fund emptied.

"Well, someone wants me dead. Someone took a shot at me a couple of hours ago. I'm pretty sure it was that man, Eldon Thatcher. I think he's working for Sean."

"You didn't report the shooting?" Jack knew he hadn't. If he had, Reyes would have called him immediately.

"No. I decided to get to safety and then contact you."

"Where are you now?" Jack demanded.

"I'd rather not say. Don't try to trace the call, either. I'm tossing my cell phone. I need to disappear for a while."

And with that, Dr. Bartolo hung up.

"Disappear," Jack mumbled. If the doctor was telling the truth and Thatcher was truly after him, then disappearing might not be possible. Dr. Bartolo could be in grave danger.

"My brother again." Alana shook her head. "His name keeps coming up at the wrong time."

"If Dr. Bartolo is telling the truth," Jack reminded her. "According to Parker, the doctor is the one with the criminal motive."

"Yes. You're right." She paused. "You think Parker will find him and make an arrest?"

Maybe. But he might not find Bartolo before Thatcher did.

The only thing remotely positive about Thatcher going after Bartolo was that it meant Joey and Alana might get a temporary reprieve. They needed it. Alana was beyond exhausted and likely missing Joey like crazy. He sure was. And both of them needed some rest.

Jack took a deep breath and took Alana's arm. "Come on. I'll fix us something to eat, and then you can get some sleep."

"I'm not really hungry."

Neither was he, but they hadn't eaten since breakfast, and here it was almost dinnertime. It wouldn't help Joey or the investigation if they starved.

Jack led her to the family-style kitchen, but when he reached the doorway, he frowned. The room was huge, sixteen feet by twenty, and had a fireplace at one end. It also had five floor-to-ceiling windows. Because those windows gave him a great view of the ranch, he'd never considered them a negative, but they were now. If Thatcher managed to get in rifle range, he'd be able to shoot right through that glass.

He went to each one and closed the blinds. Because the sun was already low in the sky, that plunged the room into near darkness. But instead of turning on the overhead light, he only switched on the dim light over the stove. It would cast fewer shadows on the blinds so it'd be harder for a shooter to pinpoint them.

"You're worried that Thatcher will use his sniper rifle again," she mumbled.

Jack didn't answer. She'd already had a too heavy dose of the truth without him confirming it.

Alana didn't look too steady on her feet, so Jack plopped her down on one of the high snack bar stools that were positioned in front of the granite counter. She caught his hand when he started to move away. Even in the darkness, he had no trouble seeing her worried eyes.

"Tell me everything's going to be all right," she said, sounding a little desperate.

"Everything will be all right." He wished he could make that true.

He brought her hand to his mouth, kissed it and placed it back in her lap. Their gazes met again. Uh-oh. Since this could quickly turn from a kiss on the hand to a real kiss, Jack stepped away.

"Juice, milk, water, iced tea?" he asked, heading for the fridge. "Or something stronger?"

"Hmmm. I'd prefer something stronger, but I'd better settle for juice."

They would both need a clear head. Still, that didn't stop him from grabbing a longneck bottle of Lone Star beer. He poured Alana a glass of orange juice and got to work on making them some sandwiches.

"You were raised here?" Alana sipped her juice and glanced around the room.

He glanced around, too, trying to see it for the first time through her eyes. It certainly wasn't fancy with its rustic floors, pine cabinets and table, but he'd added the granite counters to spruce things up a bit.

"Yes. My grandfather built this house back in the fifties, but the land has been in the Whitley family for over a hundred years."

She smiled. "The place suits you."

"Thanks. I think."

"It was a compliment. This place feels like family. Like tradition." Her smile faded when she saw the change in his expression. "What's wrong?"

He followed her gaze around the kitchen until their eyes met again. "If it feels like family, it's because of Tessie. She made this place a home for both of us. And then for Joey, too."

"Not your parents?" she questioned.

He debated how much he should tell her. "My dad's serving a life sentence in Huntsville prison. He's been there for twenty-one years. Since I was ten."

She put her hand on her chest. "I'm sorry."

He shrugged. "I'm sure you'll eventually hear talk around town. My father murdered my mother." Jack tipped his head in the direction of the west pasture. "He took her riding one day, and when they got to the creek, they got into an argument about a man he thought she'd been seeing. He got really angry and hit her in the head with a tree limb. She died instantly."

"My God."

Yeah, that'd been his reaction, too. When he'd seen it. Even now. "I'd gone for a swim that day. My father didn't know I was there, that I'd witnessed the whole thing. He told everyone my mother had died when she fell off her horse."

Obviously stunned, she leaned closer. "You actually saw him kill your mother?"

"I did." Jack had to take a deep breath. "And I testified against him. That day, I lost both my parents, and Tessie moved in so I wouldn't have to go to foster care."

He didn't have to guess what she was thinking. He knew what it was like to be abandoned, and that's why he'd been so quick to step up to take Joey.

Since this was beyond an uncomfortable situation, and one that touched on too many raw nerves, it was time for a change of topic. "I guess you were raised in a fancy house, huh?"

She just stared at him. And blinked back tears.

Great. Now he'd made her cry. "I'm sorry," he told her.

"Don't be. I'm glad you shared that with me. It gave me insight into the kind of man you are."

"I'm the kind who puts justice above all else." He cursed. That comment was a knee-jerk reaction, caused by years of overheard whispered comments. "Some people thought…think," he corrected, "that I shouldn't have turned my father in. Especially since it came out that my mother really was having an affair."

"That doesn't matter. You did the right thing," she said without hesitation.

"Yeah." He wasn't disagreeing with her, but it'd been

a damn hard decision to live with. "So, back to you," he tried again. "You were raised in a fancy house?"

For a moment, Jack didn't think she was going to let it drop. But she did. "More like middle class. My mom was from money, but her folks disapproved of my dad. When she married him, they disowned her and put their money in trust funds for Sean and me."

Jack nodded, and kept the subject going. Not just because he didn't want to discuss his parents, but because he genuinely wanted to know more about Alana. "So, how did your brother get so greedy for money?"

She took a deep breath. "I think it's because he saw how our maternal grandparents lived. And how we lived. He didn't like the disparity, and I think it made him hungry for success." But then she shook her head. "Still, there's no excuse for what he's done."

No. There wasn't. Sean had hurt her to the core.

Alana snagged his gaze again. "After we catch the person responsible, will you let me stay here awhile, so I can get to know Joey?"

"Sure. There's a guest room right next to the nursery." He waited for a pang of discomfort, jealousy or whatever emotion might come at his having to share Joey. But it didn't happen. The thought of having Alana under his roof was suddenly very appealing.

For all the wrong reasons.

To get his mind off the idea, he gulped down some beer and slid the plate with her sandwich across the counter toward her.

"Thanks," she said, looking at it. Then she looked at him.

It got so quiet that he could hear his own heartbeat pulsing in his ears, and every one of his senses seemed to home in on her.

"The sandwich," Alana mumbled. She was apparently trying to put her focus back on anything but him.

Jack tried to do the same. He thought of Thatcher. And the ranch hands who were patrolling the grounds. Of Joey. Of how close Alana and he had come to dying today. He even thought of the emotional conversation they'd just had.

None of that got his mind off Alana.

She stood slowly, and set her juice aside. She stepped toward him, brushing against the counter edge as she came to him. Alana might have started off slowly, but those last few steps were more like a leap.

She landed in his arms.

Jack took things from there, kissing her. Hard. Knowing full well that it was a stupid thing to do. And also knowing exactly where it would lead.

FINALLY!

That was Alana's first reaction when Jack's mouth came to hers. She'd been waiting for this. Wanting this. And even though it was wrong and reckless, she no longer cared. For now, for this moment, she needed Jack.

And Jack needed her.

He hooked his arm around her waist and snapped her to him. He kissed her until Alana felt as if she were about to melt.

Everything moved quickly, and neither of them tried to slow it down. The kiss was deep, hungry and intense. As was the embrace. It was a race to find some relief from the pleasure that was building inside them, a powderkeg of emotions ready to go off at any moment.

Their bodies pressed against each other, they shifted, maneuvered, tried to get closer. Off-balanced, they landed against the rim of the counter, and they bumped the plate that Jack had placed there. It went sliding across the slick surface and clanged into the granite backsplash.

He lowered his hands from her waist to her butt. Jack lifted her slightly, putting her right against his erection. She hadn't thought her need could get any stronger, but that did it. That contact was more than enough to make her feel like live fire in his hands.

"If you're going to stop—"

Alana didn't let him finish. There wouldn't be any stopping. Not on her part, anyway. Judging from Jack's reaction, he wouldn't be stopping, either.

He turned, moving her out of the kitchen and into the hall. Toward his bedroom, she realized. However, the kisses didn't stop just because they were on the move. Nor did the intimate contact. Jack scooped her up, Alana wrapped her legs around his waist and he took those wildfire kisses to her neck.

She heard herself moan. It was heavy with need. Jack moaned a little, too, when she kissed his neck. That made her wonder what else she could do to turn up his temperature.

Soon, she'd find out.

But probably not now. Her need was too frantic for foreplay or anything that involved slowing down.

He bashed his shoulder into the bedroom door to open it and stumbled toward the bed. They crashed onto the mattress with Jack landing on top of her.

"I'll do better, later," he promised.

Alana didn't know how it could get better. Every inch of her was burning for him. She hadn't felt this alive—nor this wanted—in her entire life.

Jack shoved up the stretchy top she was wearing. He flicked open the front clasp of her bra and took those melting kisses to her breasts. Even more heat blazed through her. Alana made a sound of raw pleasure that she hoped would spur Jack on.

It worked.

While he tormented her nipples, he used his knee to push up her skirt. His right leg landed between hers, right at the juncture of her thighs. Right where she wanted some pressure. And he gave it to her. He had her begging for him to do something to relieve the heat he'd built inside her.

Alana had to get off some of her clothes. Her breasts were already bare. Jack caught her panties and pulled them down her legs. But he was still fully clothed. She wanted to torment his naked the body the same way he was tormenting hers.

She fumbled with his shirt buttons, but her hands were shaking. She was shaking. Her body was screaming for her to do something. So she took a shortcut, pulled his shirt from the waist of his jeans and went exploring. She put her hands on his chest. He was solid. All man. His body was sinew and muscle built from years of working on his ranch.

He was perfect.

When her hands went lower, to his toned and rock-hard stomach, she saw pleasure flicker through his jaw muscles. He made a husky, throaty sound.

She went lower still, and since he was driving her crazy kissing her nipples, she decided to turn the tables on him. She somehow got his belt undone and his jeans unzipped.

Before she could get her hands in his boxers, however, Jack upped the insanity. He shoved aside her panties, made his way down her body and gave her a kiss she was certain she would never forget.

Alana saw stars.

She couldn't wait any longer.

She grabbed him and pulled him back up. She got her hand inside his boxers, and touched him. He was huge, hard and just as ready as she was. Her touch made him curse.

He was a little rough and obviously in a hurry. She didn't care. Alana shoved her heels against the mattress so that she could help Jack maneuver them toward the headboard. Except that wasn't his goal. He was after the nightstand. And after fumbling around in the drawer, he produced a condom. Good thing. She certainly hadn't remembered the concept of safe sex.

They didn't even take off the rest of their clothes. Every second was torture.

Until he pushed inside her.

Alana stilled, to savor the moment and the sensations that speared through her. But the stillness didn't last. It couldn't. Her body demanded satisfaction.

They found a rhythm that was as old as time and yet it felt to her as if this was too intense, too special to have been experienced by anyone before.

His eyes met hers. He continued to move inside her, one long thrust after another. She watched his face and saw what this was doing to him. Alana was certain that her own out-of-control need was mirrored in the depth of his gunmetal-blue eyes.

She said his name on a rise of breath. “Jack.”

“Alana.” It barely had sound, and yet she could feel his emotion as he plunged them both closer and closer to the edge.

Mercy, she wanted to let go. To feel. To fly.

He didn’t make her wait long. He moved faster. Deeper. His eyes, narrowed. His breath gusted against her face.

And when Alana took that leap, when Jack pushed her over the edge, she didn’t hold anything back. She let herself go. Felt herself close around him.

Felt herself shatter.

Jack lowered his head. He kissed her so gently that it stunned her even more than the raw pleasure that was coursing through her body. That kiss cut right through the passion-induced haze, and she saw everything clearly. Too clearly.

Oh, no.

She’d let herself fall in love with Jack.

The question was—what was she going to do about it?

Chapter Fourteen

Jack stood in the shower and hoped the scalding hot water would help the knotted muscles in his neck and back. It was too much to hope that it'd help the rest of him relax. He needed a head examination. He'd hauled Alana off to bed and had sex with her.

Great sex.

He'd known it was inevitable, that they would eventually give in to the heat that flamed between them, but he also knew that it would complicate things beyond belief.

What the hell was he supposed to do now?

Invite Alana to move in? That would solve their custody issues temporarily, but it wouldn't solve anything else. Willow Ridge was a small, conservative town, and while no one would begrudge him having an affair, it was a different thing entirely to have Alana live with him. He didn't want Alana, Tessie or Joey subjected to that kind of gossip. Which led him back to his original question.

What was he supposed to do?

Before he could go through his slim options, he

heard a knock. He reacted fast, because he'd told Alana to alert him if there even a hint that something might be wrong.

He jumped from the shower, reached for a towel and stopped in midreach when the door flew open.

It was Alana.

She had the phone in her hand. "Sorry. It's Sheriff Tanner. He wants us to know that they all arrived safely."

That was good news, and he was glad she'd delivered it right away.

But she was looking at him as if she wanted him all over again, and even though he'd just had that argument with himself, Jack wanted her again, too.

"The sheriff, uh, wants to talk to you," Alana said, passing him the phone.

Jack grabbed a towel and draped it around his waist before taking the phone. What he didn't do was move away from Alana. She didn't move away from him, either. She stood, just inches away. So close he could take in her scent.

This was going to get hot fast.

"It's Jack," he answered. "Alana said you arrived." He didn't mention the location and wouldn't, just in case someone had managed to tap into the conversation, but Jack knew Sheriff Tanner had taken Joey and Tessie to a safe house.

"Everything went as planned," Tanner assured him. "Just call when you're ready for me to bring 'em back."

"Oh, I will. Thanks, Beck."

Jack considered drawing out the conversation, just so it would keep his mind off sex. But that wasn't going to happen. Not with Alana so close he could practically taste her.

So that's what he did.

He clicked the end-call button. With the phone in his right hand, he curved his left hand around the back of her neck and eased her to him. The towel fell, leaving him with very visible proof of how much he wanted her.

He kissed her, slow and easy. Something that'd been sorely lacking in that crazy frenzy on the bed. He took his time, savoring her, letting the taste of her slide right through him.

She pulled back and ran her tongue over her bottom lip. "Hmmm. That was nice," she murmured.

Yeah, and he was about to make it a lot *nicer*.

But Alana didn't exactly cooperate. She pulled back, stared at him and opened her mouth to speak. Judging from the suddenly serious expression that swept over her, this wasn't going to be something he wanted to hear.

Then she stopped and glanced around. "I think I smell smoke."

Jack lifted his head and sniffed. Alarmed, he sniffed again. There was definitely a trace of smoke in the air.

"Did you put something on the stove?" he asked, hoping she had.

"No."

There was no need to panic—one of the ranch hands could be burning some brush—but he couldn't stop that jolt of adrenaline.

Alana turned toward the door. "I'll check the kitchen."

But Jack caught her arm. "Wait. I'll go with you."

He was certain that he'd frightened her, but he had no choice. In case something had gone wrong, he didn't want her out there alone. He grabbed his clothes and dressed as fast as he could. He was strapping on his shoulder holster just as his cell phone rang. He snatched it from his pocket.

"It's Deacon," his ranch hand said. With just those two words, Jack could hear the concern in the man's voice. He didn't have to wait long to understand why. "You need to get out of there now! The house is on fire."

"A fire? Where? How?"

"Don't know the how part yet, but it's on the west side of the house."

The kitchen was on the west side. Jack still held out hope that this was caused by something electrical. But with Eldon Thatcher on the loose, he had to anticipate the worst.

"Make sure no one's out there with a rifle," Jack ordered, though with the darkness, that might not be possible.

"Will do. I'll also call the fire department," Deacon said. "You just get yourself out of there."

Jack stabbed the end-call button, shoved the phone in his pocket and drew his weapon. With his left hand, he caught Alana's arm and got them moving. There were plenty of ways to exit the house, but Jack wondered if any of them would be safe.

It certainly wasn't safe to stay put.

There were already wispy coils of smoke in his bedroom and in the hallway, and when he glanced in the direction of the kitchen, he could see that the smoke was considerably thicker there. He could feel the heat, too, which meant the fire was probably already eating its way through the house.

"Stay behind me," he instructed Alana and hoped she wouldn't give him an argument. She didn't. Like him, she was aware of the possibility that this could be some ploy by Thatcher to draw them out.

Unfortunately, it would work.

He couldn't keep Alana inside, but by God, he could do everything within his power to keep her from being an easy target.

"We're going out the back door?" she asked when he took her in that direction.

"Yeah."

It was a gamble. But he wanted to get Alana out and to the nearest barn so she'd have protection.

He thought of Joey and was damn glad he'd sent his son away. As bad as this could be, he wouldn't have wanted Joey anywhere near this.

Alana coughed from the smoke, and Jack used his hand to whip it away. It was a lost cause. The smoke was thicker in the back of the house, and he felt as if it were choking him. Still, he got them to the back door.

He stopped and pressed his hand to the wood. It was cool to the touch, which meant there wasn't a blaze on the other side. But the fire wasn't his greatest fear. Outside, there were plenty of places for a shooter to hide. If Thatcher had made it onto the ranch—and that wouldn't be that hard to do if he'd come in on foot—then he could be anywhere.

"Your home," Alana mumbled. "It's being destroyed."

There was nothing he could do about it now.

The ranch hands were no doubt assembling so they could use a hose to try to battle the flames. Deacon had already called the fire department, but Jack had to be honest with himself. The ranch wasn't close to town. It could take the volunteer fire department at least twenty minutes to get to them, and if the blaze was as big as he thought it was, a hose wasn't going to do much.

Jack eased open the door and looked out. There were floodlights on at the corners of the house, and there was another light on the front exterior of the barn. Those along with the moonlight made it possible for him to see. But he didn't see the gunman, only the ranch hands scrambling to the fire.

"When we get out, run," Jack instructed. "I don't want you out in the open any longer than necessary."

She nodded and because he knew they both could use it, he pressed a quick kiss on her mouth. In the same motion, he tightened his grip, took a deep breath and barreled down the steps.

They didn't even make it to the bottom before a bullet slammed into the porch pillar next to Alana's head.

ALANA HEARD THE BLAST.

Her first thought was that the fire had blown out a window. But a split second later, her fears were confirmed. Jack pushed her to the side, practically tackling her, and they both crashed hard onto the porch.

Another bullet slammed into the wall.

If Jack hadn't reacted so quickly, she would have been shot. Or worse.

Latching on to her, Jack scrambled behind one of the white round porch pillars. Some shrubs were the only other cover they had. She turned her head and looked at the house to see if they could make it back inside.

Not a chance.

The orange and red flames were licking against the kitchen windows. The fire hadn't consumed the house yet, but the smoke would have already made the air inside unbreathable. Still, they couldn't stay put, because the fire would eventually reach the porch.

They'd be caught in the middle. Death by fire. Or death by bullets.

Alana didn't want either.

They had to survive this for Joey's sake. She refused to let whoever had done this take away her son's chance at having a good life.

From the west side of the house, she heard the frantic shouts of the ranch hands. She didn't know how many of them there were, but hopefully they were all armed. She could also hear water running. Someone was spraying it onto those flames.

Another bullet fired at them. This one broke the window just above their heads and showered them with glass, ash and smoke.

"He's on the roof of the barn," Jack called out, so the ranch hands would know where to aim. Within seconds, someone on the side of the house was shooting at the barn.

"Can you see who's on the roof?" she asked.

Jack shook his head. "I know he's there because of the direction of the shots." But they both knew it was probably Thatcher, and he wouldn't stop until they stopped him.

More shots slammed into the porch, one of them skidding across the wooden planks. It sent splinters flying everywhere. As dangerous as the bullets, splinters and glass were, however, it was the fire that would soon be the most deadly threat. Flames shot out of the gaping holes in the glass, and a gust of black smoke wafted right at them.

Jack adjusted their positions, pushing her facedown onto the porch, and he hovered over her so that he was using his body as a shield. Alana didn't approve of him putting her life ahead of his. She wanted to do something to help.

But what?

"Can you throw us a rifle?" she called out to the ranch hands. She couldn't see them. They had taken cover on the side of the house, but if the guys could get them a rifle, they'd have some way to return fire and protect themselves.

Several moments later, a rifle skittered across the porch toward them. Jack reached for it but had to jerk back his hand when a bullet slammed right next to them.

The ranch hands retaliated. She heard at least two shooters take aim at the barn. The bullets smacked into the side and the metal roof. It was just the diversion they needed. Jack rolled to the side, thrust his gun into her hand and snatched up the rifle.

"Fire now!" Jack shouted to the ranch hands.

They did. Jack, too.

The blasts were deafening and nonstop.

Jack came up on one knee, took aim and fired.

Alana wanted to grab him, to pull him back on the porch floor where it was safer, but just like that, the shots stopped.

Terrified, she scrambled so she could see Jack and make sure he hadn't been shot. But relief flooded through her when she didn't see any blood.

Jack didn't move. He knelt there, aiming at the barn. A moment later, she realized why.

She lifted her head just slightly and saw the man. He was dressed like a ranch hand, but even from the distance and near darkness, Alana could see that it was Eldon Thatcher. And unlike Jack, he was bleeding.

Thatcher staggered, and somehow got to his feet despite his injury and the pitched angle of the roof. Alana watched in horror as Thatcher lifted his rifle and took aim at Jack.

"No!" she screamed.

But it was too late. As the sound blasted through the air, she felt everything inside her go numb.

"Jack?" she called out.

"I'm fine," he assured her.

And he was. Thatcher hadn't fired. Jack had.

She snapped her attention back to Thatcher in time to see the rifle drop from his hands. He crumpled into a heap, and as if in slow motion, his body slid from the roof and plunged to the ground below.

Alana didn't have time to feel any relief.

"Come on," Jack said. He grabbed her hand and pulled her to her feet.

Her legs were wobbly. Her lungs felt clogged and heavy. Every step was a challenge, but she somehow made it off that porch.

It wasn't a second too soon.

The fire blazed across the porch, and the roof that had protected them just moments earlier came crashing down right at them.

Chapter Fifteen

Jack pulled Alana into the back yard, fighting to get her away from the collapsing porch.

Cinders, ash and debris spewed in every direction, and that caused the ranch hands to scatter, as well. The porch seemed to groan as it crashed into a burning heap. But Jack didn't even look back. He kept his attention on Thatcher. Even though the man appeared to be dead, Jack wasn't taking any chances.

"Stay down," Jack warned Alana.

He positioned her behind a pair of twin oaks that had a hammock stretched between them. He wanted her to be protected.

While the ranch hands got to work dousing the fire, Jack approached Thatcher, keeping his rifle aimed.

"Need me to call for an ambulance?" Deacon yelled.

Jack went closer. "No." It was clear that Thatcher was dead. But just in case, Jack knelt down and pressed his fingers to the man's neck.

No pulse.

"But you can call the medical examiner," Jack relayed to Deacon. "And get Reyes out here." He would need his deputy to tie up loose ends, since Jack had been the shooter.

While they were waiting for him, Jack knew he had to work to contain that blaze. If not, the whole house would go up in flames.

He turned to hurry back to the house, but then he saw Alana. Her face was colorless, despite the intense heat from the fire.

"He's dead?" she asked.

Jack nodded and went to her.

She blew out a long breath and nodded, as she stared at the man's lifeless body. "Good."

He understood her relief. Jack hated that he'd just killed a man. But Thatcher would have just kept coming if Jack hadn't stopped him.

Because there wasn't time for anything more, Jack brushed a kiss on her cheek, propped his rifle against the oak and took his gun from her. He reholstered it and got busy. He raced toward the barn, where there was another hose, turned it on and hurried with it toward the house.

Alana grabbed a blanket from the hammock and tried to beat down the flames that were flickering into the yard. It was a good move. The grass was dry in patches, and he didn't want the fire to spread to any of the outbuildings.

In the distance, Jack heard sirens. Thank God. The fire engine was close by, and even though there'd been a lot of damage, they might still be able to save the house.

"Should I try to go inside and get out anything?" Deacon asked.

"No way." It was tempting. A lot of his life was in that house. Joey's life, too. But things could be replaced, and Jack didn't want anyone else dying today.

The fire engine came screaming into the driveway in front of the house, and Jack hurried to it so he could get them maneuvered in the right direction. Not that they could miss the fire. The black coil of smoke rising into the air was a telltale sign.

The volunteer firemen were all men he knew. Friends and neighbors barreled off the engine, ready to respond. It didn't take long before they had their hose connected to the emergency tap, and they began to spray the house.

Jack glanced at Alana. She was still battling those grass fires, and he turned to help her. But then he spotted another vehicle approaching. It was Reyes.

"Thatcher's dead," Jack told the deputy when he jumped from his cruiser. Reyes already had his gun drawn as if he'd expected the worst.

"The M.E.'s on the way," Reyes let him know. "We might have another problem, though. Dr. Bartolo's missing. He's not at home or at the hospital. His cleaning lady was at his house and I asked her to look around, to see if anything was missing. She said the gun from his nightstand was gone."

Yes. The doctor. Jack would have to deal with him soon. After all, the man had been involved in an illegal diamond deal, and he might even have had a part in what had happened to Alana. Heck, for that matter, he could have been the one who sent Thatcher after them.

And with that thought, Jack froze.

What if Dr. Bartolo came after Alana?

Jack raced toward the back of the house, and his heart dropped. She wasn't there where he'd last seen her.

"Deacon, where's Alana?"

Deacon fired some glances around and shrugged. "I thought she was with you."

Jack cursed and tried not to panic. The whole yard was chaotic with the firefighters and his ranch hands. There were nearly a dozen people centered on the activity, and Alana could be among them.

But she wasn't.

"Alana?" he called out.

Nothing.

Jack raced to the oaks and the hammock, and spotted the charred blanket on the ground. She'd been using it to beat out the flames, but there it was, tossed aside. And no Alana in sight.

"Check the barn," he instructed Reyes. His deputy had already drawn his weapon, and Jack did the same. He prayed he wouldn't have to use it.

While Reyes went in the direction of the barn, Jack headed for the east side of the house. Away from fire. Away from the chaos.

He raced around the corner. No Alana.

With his breath gusting and adrenaline shooting through him, he stopped, listened and prayed that all was well. But in his gut, he knew something was wrong.

"Alana?" he called out again.

Still nothing.

Where was she? Where could she have gone? But the real question was, had Dr. Bartolo taken the gun from his house so he could use it on Alana?

Jack heard a sound.

It was like a muffled scream. A cry for help. He sprinted in the direction of that sound. It'd come from the front of the house, but Alana wasn't there.

With panic rising in his throat, he glanced all around. At the fire engine. The deputy's cruiser. His work truck. His damaged SUV that he'd parked out front. No one was around the vehicles. But when he looked up the road, he spotted a dark blue car stopped just on the other side of the open cattle gate.

Jack had seen that car before.

In fact, it'd been at the ranch earlier—when Sean, Margaret and Parker had arrived for their little visit.

He kept his gun ready and headed in the direction of the vehicle. There was a dark tint on the windows, and he couldn't see if anyone was inside.

God, had one of the three taken Alana?

Jack was within ten yards or so of the car when the engine roared on. He raised his gun and aimed, but he couldn't fire. He couldn't risk hitting Alana if she was in there.

"Alana?" he called out again.

He didn't expect an answer and didn't get one, but he knew she was inside. He just knew it. And he also knew the person who had her was up to no good.

"Get out of the car," he ordered, bracing his shooting wrist with his left hand.

But no one got out. The driver, concealed behind that dark tint, gunned the engine.

And drove right at Jack.

ALANA BLINKED AND TRIED TO SEE what was happening.

What was wrong with her?

Everything was hazy again, just as it'd been while she was imprisoned at Sauder. She'd been drugged then. Had someone drugged her now?

She forced herself to concentrate, but everything was swimming in and out of focus. She couldn't see anything clearly. She thought she might be in a car. And someone had put her there.

Who?

Someone sat beside her, in the driver's seat, and she could hear the sound of the engine. Then it hit her. She was being kidnapped.

She groaned and tried to reach out to strike the person, to fight back, but her meager attack only resulted in a light slap to the person's arm.

Again, she tried to focus so she could see who'd taken her, but her eyes wouldn't cooperate. The dizziness was overwhelming and made her sick to her stomach. Added to that, there was a sickeningly sweet taste in her mouth.

The car lurched forward.

Her arm and shoulder rammed into the dashboard, and the pain was instant. But that impact told her something critical.

She wasn't wearing a seat belt. Nor was she tied up. That meant she could escape.

Someone called out her name.

"Alana?" She heard it clearly. A shout.

Jack.

Judging from his frantic tone, he knew that she was in danger.

She tried to answer him, but failed.

The car was the last place she wanted to be. Alana groped for the handle to open the door. She felt the window. Then the leather strip below it. Finally, her fingers closed around the metal lever.

But someone stopped her.

A hand latched on to her wrist and jerked her hand from the lever.

Furious and frantic that she'd failed, Alana tried to fight back at the fierce grip her kidnapper had on her. But her arms were weak, practically limp. As was the rest of her body. Her fight ended with her hands dropping into her lap.

The car swerved to the left, causing her hip to slam into the gearshift. What was going on? Was the kidnapper trying to get away from Jack?

Alana blinked several times, and saw something. Jack. He jumped to the side of the road. If he hadn't done that, the car would have plowed right into him. The blurriness returned in spades, and even though she couldn't see exactly what was happening, she was almost positive that the driver turned around to go after Jack again.

"No!" she yelled.

She grabbed for the steering wheel. It was a huge risk. Because she couldn't see, she could do more harm than good and cause the vehicle to hit Jack. Still, she had to try. She had to do something, because this monster might hurt Jack. And once he had Jack out of the way, God knows where the kidnapper would take her. Or what he would do to her.

She doubted he'd keep her alive very long.

There was the whirring sound of a window being lowered, and hot muggy air rushed into the car. Suddenly, the sounds were a lot clearer. She could hear Jack again. He was shouting for her to get out. So Alana tried again. She reached for the door handle.

But the blast stopped her.

After the shoot-out they'd just had with Thatcher, she knew that sound.

A shot being fired.

Her captor had shot at Jack.

She scrambled to get into a sitting position so she could see what was going on. But dizziness didn't allow her to see much, just the fuzzy image of the person seated beside her. A man, she thought. Outside, there in the darkness, she also thought she saw Jack. He was alive, and scrambling toward the car.

Alana called out his name again. A warning, for him to stop before he got shot. She didn't want to die, but dying wasn't the worst thing that could happen to her. The worst would be for Jack to die while trying to save her.

"I love you," she said. But it came out mumbled. Jack probably couldn't hear her, but she wanted him to know how she felt about him.

Beside her, her captor laughed. Maybe he was amused that she was pouring out her heart. That made her angry. It made her want to lash out at him for trying to hurt Jack.

But another shot sounded.

The blast tore through the car, but even over the roar it created in her ears, Alana heard the rev of the car engine. The vehicle spun around, and the driver floored the accelerator.

She glanced around, and even through the haze and the darkness in her mind, she realized they were speeding away from the ranch.

That couldn't happen.

What if Jack was hurt and bleeding back there? He

might need medical attention. “Stop!” she managed to shout at her captor. “We have to go back.”

He laughed again.

Alana gathered up all the energy and anger that she could. She balled her hands into fists, turned and began to pummel him. Her hands and arms might have been weak, but she tried to go after his face so that her blows might do some good.

She felt cold metal jam against her left temple.

“Stop, or you’ll die right here,” he growled. “And then I’ll go after your son.”

Oh, God.

She stared at the man. Slowly, very slowly, the dizziness faded so that she could hone in on his face.

“How about another hit of chloroform?” he asked. “That’ll make you cooperate.”

Chloroform. So that’s why she couldn’t move or think clearly. That’s what he’d used to get her into the car.

And now he had her.

Chapter Sixteen

Jack jumped into his work truck and thanked God that the keys were in the ignition.

He started the engine, put on his seat belt and drove off in pursuit. He'd seen the face of Alana's kidnapper, and he knew this would be no easy battle.

Special Agent Parker Howell knew how to fight.

And win.

The SOB had Alana. And when Parker had shot at him and tried to run him down, the agent had made it crystal clear that he wasn't a good guy. Jack figured it was only a matter of time before he tried to kill Alana.

If he hadn't tried already.

Parker's car kicked up some dust as it barreled down the narrow road that led away from the ranch. Jack needed to keep a visual on the car's taillights because once Parker reached the highway, he could go in either direction, and there'd be no dust trail to follow. Jack didn't intend to lose the man. He vowed he'd stop Parker and get Alana safely back.

Jack kept a firm grip on the steering wheel and took

out his phone to call Reyes so he could request backup. But it didn't work.

No signal.

There were plenty of reception dead spots around the ranch, but this shouldn't have been one of them. Did that mean Parker had somehow jammed the phones so they couldn't be used? Probably. As an FBI agent, Parker would have had access to that type of equipment. But that wouldn't stop Jack, either. He kept the accelerator pushed to the floor, and tried not to think of what Alana was going through. She was no doubt scared out of her mind. But she would almost certainly know that he would come after her.

But then, Parker would know it, too.

That thought had no sooner formed in his head than he turned a sharp curve. The sides of the road were thick with trees on each side, and along with the darkness, it made it impossible to see what was ahead until he was already deep into the turn.

Parker's car was right in the middle of the road.

Jack slammed on his brakes, but he knew there wasn't enough distance between him and the car. He was about to crash into it, and that couldn't happen. He would hit the passenger's side, right where Alana was sitting.

Hell.

Parker had parked the car there so he could set Jack up to kill her.

Jack jerked the steering wheel to the left, praying that it would be in time to miss Parker's car. It was. Barely. His truck slammed into the back end of the car, knocking it forward but leaving it intact. Jack didn't have time to celebrate his victory, though, because his truck left the road and went flying down the steep embankment.

A tree limb smashed into his windshield, cracking the glass so that he couldn't see what was ahead. But he knew. There were more trees—big sprawling oaks—and a creek. This was the shallow side. He wouldn't drown if he hit the water, but an impact with trees and the limestone boulders in the creek bed could be fatal.

Jack braced himself for the collision. He didn't have to wait long. The truck plowed into an outcropping of rocks, and that propelled the right side of his vehicle into a tree.

The jolt snapped him forward, and the airbag slammed into him.

Jack didn't waste any time assessing if he was hurt. He elbowed the airbag aside and threw open the door. He hit the ground running toward Parker's car and kept his gun ready. He couldn't just open fire and risk hitting Alana, so he had to choose his shots carefully.

His knee throbbed as he ran up the embankment. He'd hit it during the wreck but didn't care. Nothing was going to stop him from making it to Alana.

He slowed when he got to the top and tried to keep low. He walked toward Parker's car. The road was eerily quiet, with just the sound of the summer breeze rifling through the tree branches and the soft ripple of the creek flowing over the rocks. The car sat there, surrounded by the pitchy darkness.

"This ends now," Jack shouted to Parker. "I want you to release Alana."

No answer.

That could mean Parker was sitting there, waiting to ambush him, but Jack couldn't just wait him out. The car was still in the middle of the road, and if any other fire department vehicles came racing this way, they'd plow right into it. He had to get Alana out of there.

"Parker?" Jack called out.

Still nothing.

Jack eased closer, with his gun still ready, and he looked inside the darkly tinted windows.

He cursed.

The car was empty.

Jack dropped to the ground and not a second too soon.

A bullet came right at him.

He scrambled to the back of the car so he could use it as cover. He needed to get off the road, and to Alana, and staying put wouldn't accomplish that.

Another shot fired. Then another.

The shots came from the opposite side of the road from where he'd crashed.

Jack lifted his head slightly and looked around. He didn't see any sign of Parker or Alana, but they had to be out there somewhere. What he needed was a little visual help.

Staying low, he made his way back to the passenger's-side door, reached up and grabbed the handle. The door was unlocked. That was a lucky break. He opened it and reached inside to turn on the headlights. The high beams were aimed right at the trees where Parker was hiding.

Jack saw a flash of movement. But he had to duck back down because another bullet came his way. This one smacked into the car just above his head.

"Parker, you're only digging your own grave," Jack shouted. "Surrender now. You know I won't let you get away with this."

Jack waited for an answer for several long moments.

"Okay," Parker yelled back. "I'll trade Alana for a head start. You get her, and I get back in my car and drive away. You all right with that?"

He wasn't. Jack didn't want Parker getting away. But Alana came first. Once he had her back, then he could go after Parker.

"Let's do this," Jack agreed.

"First, put down your gun," Parker shouted.

Jack cursed under his breath. "Not without some kind of assurance that Alana is all right." Even then, he was taking a huge risk because Parker could just shoot him.

In fact, that was probably Parker's plan.

The agent wouldn't want to leave any witnesses, especially a sheriff and a former hostage. No, this was almost certainly a trap to draw Jack out so that Parker could kill him and then hightail it out of there with Alana. But that did make Jack wonder…why had Parker kept her alive?

What did he want with her?

"Alana's fine," Parker insisted. "A little woozy from the chloroform, but she doesn't have a scratch on her. Cooperate, and she'll stay that way."

Jack wasn't untouched by that threat, but if he allowed himself to be killed, then Alana would be at Parker's mercy.

"I want to see her now," Jack countered.

The silence returned. So did the fear. Not for himself…Jack was terrified for Alana.

Finally, there was some movement in the trees, and a second later, he saw Alana. Alive, thank God. And

Parker was right—she didn't appear to be harmed. Well, except the look of terror on her face.

Parker had positioned her in front of him to use as a human shield. He had his left hand squeezed over her mouth, and his right hand held a gun pointed directly to her head.

"Now you've seen her," Parker said. "Put down your gun."

Jack stood there, debating. He couldn't put his gun down. But he had to do something. "Bring her closer so I can get a better look at her."

From the way Parker's mouth tightened, it was obvious he was having a debate with himself, as well. Still, the man walked closer and stopped just at the edge of the embankment. With the slope, Alana was still a good fifteen feet away. Much too far for Jack to try to lunge at the man.

"Put down your gun," Parker repeated.

"I will. Just as soon as I'm sure she's okay. Take your hand from her mouth so she can speak." Jack eased closer. Just a step.

"There's no reason for her to speak. She's fine. And you're stalling."

Jack took another step. "I want to hear from her own lips that you haven't hurt her."

"I haven't," Parker snapped. He jabbed the gun harder against her temple. "But I will if you don't stop this. Put down your gun now!"

Jack managed another step, but he figured that was as far as he could go. Parker already seemed ready to snap. He certainly wasn't the composed agent who'd visited Jack earlier. So even though he was still about ten feet away, Jack would have to risk making a dive for Parker if the man showed any indication that he was going to shoot Alana.

"Okay, I'm putting down my gun." Jack started to lean down.

But then he saw Alana.

She frantically shook her head.

That garnered her another jab from Parker's gun, and he cursed at her. As hard as it was to do, Jack ignored that latest jab and followed the direction of Alana's gaze toward the woods.

The headlights didn't illuminate that area, but Jack fastened his attention there, and saw something move.

"Get down!" Alana shouted, tearing Parker's hand from her mouth.

Jack dived to the asphalt just as someone fired a shot from the pitch-black woods.

ALANA KNEW HER WARNING WAS TOO LATE. The shots had already started.

She saw Jack hit the ground and prayed that the bullet hadn't found its intended target.

Parker took aim at Jack while he shoved his hand back over her mouth and tried to drag her back behind the trees. Alana was still dizzy and weak from the drug, but she couldn't let that stop her. She had to help Jack survive or they would both die right here in these woods.

She rammed her elbow into Parker's stomach. It didn't pack much of a wallop, but it did cause him to move back slightly. It was just enough for her to turn and grab his wrist so that he, too, couldn't shoot at Jack. One shooter was more than enough.

"Alana!" she heard Jack say.

It was a warning for her to be careful. But she didn't have the luxury of being careful now.

The shots from the other side stopped as she hoped they would. But Parker was still a huge threat.

She dug her fingernails into Parker's wrist and drew blood. But it wasn't enough to stop him from hitting her. He slapped her with his left hand and sent her staggering backward. Alana felt herself falling, and there was nothing she could do to stop it. She crashed into some thick underbrush, and her head smacked hard against the rocky ground.

Jack called out her name again, and she tried to get up. Thorns and sharp brush cut into her hands, but still she tried.

Parker raised his gun, and aimed at Jack. Alana struggled even harder to get up and managed to fight her way out of the underbrush. There was no time for her to yell for Jack to get down, to take cover.

She was too late.

Jack launched himself at Parker, and the two men crashed into each other. She heard the sickening sounds of bone and muscle colliding.

She got to her feet, somehow, and tried to help, but the men were in a fight for their lives. Worse, they maneuvered themselves out of the line of the headlights, and in the darkness, she couldn't see who was winning.

Alana grabbed a fist-size rock from the ground and went toward the fight. It wasn't much of a weapon, considering that both men were still armed, but she might get lucky and land a blow on Parker's shooting hand.

"I can't let you do that," someone said.

Margaret.

Alana's heart went to her knees. She looked up at the top of the embankment and spotted the woman with the rifle. It had a night scope, and even though Margaret wasn't holding the weapon with much confidence, it didn't take a mountain of confidence to kill.

Just seconds before Parker had stopped his car in the middle of the road, he'd called someone and told them to "get ready." In that moment Alana had realized that he had a partner, but she hadn't thought it would be Margaret. She'd expected her brother or Dr. Bartolo to be positioned in those woods.

"Don't move," Margaret warned.

Alana shook her head. "I can't let Parker hurt Jack."

Margaret shook her head, as well. "And I can't let you and Jack escape."

Alana glanced at Jack just as he landed a hard punch to Parker's jaw. Jack was winning, but even if he managed to subdue Parker, they had to deal with Margaret.

"What's in this for you?" Alana asked. She kept her eye on Margaret's trigger finger while she tried to inch her way to Jack.

"I won't go to jail."

"Don't be so sure about that." Alana managed another step.

"I didn't know Parker kept you at Sauder illegally. I swear, I didn't know, but a judge will never believe that."

"He will if I testify for you."

Parker shouted, "Shut up!"

But Margaret shook her head again. "Parker said I can have a fresh start in Mexico. He gave me money."

"Money he stole from me." Alana took another step toward Jack and tightened her grip on the rock. "You can testify against him, Margaret. You might not have to go to jail at all."

It was obvious that Parker was the dirty one here. She didn't know all the details of what he'd done, but Margaret could provide some answers.

But for now, Alana had to do something about Parker.

She prayed she was reading Margaret right. The woman didn't seem to have murder on her mind. Yes, she had the rifle pointed right at Alana, but she was making no moves to stop her. So Alana turned toward the men, just as Parker managed to aim his gun at Jack.

She saw Parker's hand tense, and knew that unlike Margaret, he would shoot to kill. So she did the only thing she could.

Alana dived at them.

The rock fell as she latched on to Parker's hand. But she could only hold him for a few seconds before he shoved her aside.

But with Parker's right hand temporarily occupied fighting her off, Jack took full advantage. He bashed his fist into Parker's jaw twice. The bone-crushing blows echoed through the woods, as did the feral growl of pain that came from the man's throat.

Jack didn't let Parker regain control. Neither did Alana. She snatched away his gun and scrambled away so that Parker couldn't grab her again and use her as cover. Jack shoved his gun right against Parker's head.

"Move and you die," Jack said. It wasn't just a threat. His tone, tight jaw and fierce expression made it a promise.

Parker stared at Jack, and for one horrifying moment, Alana thought he might force Jack to kill him. But he only cursed, and his hands fell against the ground.

"Well?" Jack called out.

Not to her, Alana realized. He was speaking to Margaret. Even though he'd been embroiled in that fight with Parker, he had still realized what was going on.

"Put down the rifle," Jack insisted.

The woman stood there, her rifle still pointed at Alana. Alana had Parker's gun, but by the time she aimed it, Margaret would have plenty of time to fire.

Plenty of time to kill.

Or to allow Parker to get away.

Alana glanced at Jack. He hadn't been shot, but there was blood streaming from a gash on his head. After crashing into that tree and the fight he'd just had with Parker, he might have injuries that needed immediate attention. That wasn't going to happen until Margaret was out of the way.

"You want to die, too?" Jack asked Margaret. "Because that's what'll happen if you don't put down that rifle."

Alana held her breath and prayed. But she also got ready, just in case. She slid her finger over the trigger and tried to prepare herself for whatever might happen next.

Margaret lowered the rifle.

Jack hauled Parker to his feet, but kept his gun on him. "Get behind us," he instructed Alana.

She did. But she also kept her finger on the trigger.

"You might as well kill me," Parker grumbled. "I can't go to jail. You know what they do to former agents inside a prison? I wouldn't last a week."

Jack got him moving toward the embankment.

"You should have thought of that before you shut Alana away in that institution you created so you could steal her money."

"I had to have her money. I had people to pay off. The wrong people."

"If all you wanted was my money, then why try to kill me?" Alana wanted to know.

Parker stopped at the embankment and looked over his shoulder at her. The corner of his mouth lifted in a warped half smile. There was blood on his lips and teeth, and that only added to his sinister expression. "You honestly don't know?"

"Know what?"

He laughed. "Now, this is true irony. I set up that diamond deal, and you started asking too many questions. You figured out what I'd done, that I was the seller. That I'd stolen the diamonds from evidence storage. I hired Thatcher, sent him after you and paid him well. He failed. Three times."

She shook her head. "But I didn't know you had set up the deal. I didn't remember it."

"That's the irony. But that doesn't mean you wouldn't have remembered, eventually. I couldn't take that risk."

Jack shoved Parker up the first few steps of the embankment. It was steep, and both men staggered to keep their footing.

Everything seemed to move in slow motion. Parker turned, slamming his arm into Jack's chest. Jack fell backward, while Parker reached into the back waist of his pants and pulled out a small handgun. His backup weapon.

An oily smile twisted Parker's bloody mouth as he

took aim at her. Alana didn't have time to react. She could only brace herself for a fatal shot.

The sound of the shot blasted through the air.

Her heart jumped from the jolt of adrenaline, and she got a split-second glimpse of what it was like to die. Her biggest regret was that she hadn't had time to be a real mother to Joey. Her son wouldn't remember her. He wouldn't know how precious he was to her. But she also regretted that Jack hadn't heard her when she'd said "I love you."

But the impact never came.

Parker hadn't fired.

Jack had.

Parker's body jerked violently, and she saw the blank expression in his eyes as he tumbled face-first to the ground.

Jack quickly took aim at Margaret. The woman's mouth was open in a silent scream. The rifle dropped from her hand.

Without taking his gaze off Margaret, Jack reached down and put his fingers to Parker's neck. "He's dead," he told Alana.

"Dead," she repeated.

Relief rushed through her and robbed her of any energy she had left. Jack made it to her in one step and pulled her into his arms before she collapsed.

Chapter Seventeen

Eighteen.

That was the number of cuts and scratches Jack counted on Alana's body. The majority were on her hands and arms, the result of Parker shoving her into the thorny underbrush. There was also one on her forehead. Another on her chin.

All her injuries had been examined and were being cleaned by a med tech. The E.R. doctor had insisted that none were serious. Maybe the physical injuries weren't. But Jack wasn't so sure about the mental ones.

Alana had been shot at, drugged and taken hostage. And to top it all off, she'd had to witness him kill two men. Jack wondered how many sleepless nights that would cost her.

Wearing a badge didn't make him immune to the sickening feeling that he was responsible for two men no longer being alive. But he hadn't had an alternative. He knew that, and he would have to learn to live with any feelings of guilt.

Alana winced a little as the tech dabbed at the scrape on her knee with antiseptic, but he stayed back and let the tech do his job. Jack was afraid that if he went to Alana now and pulled her into his arms she'd fall apart. Her raw emotions were simmering right below the surface.

He heard footsteps behind him, turned and spotted Reyes walking up the E.R. corridor toward him. His deputy had gotten stuck tying up all the loose ends because Alana had insisted that Jack receive medical attention for his own cuts and scrapes. Jack had agreed because that was the only way Alana would go to the hospital. If she'd had her way, she would still be waiting at his office for Sheriff Tanner to return with Joey and Tessie.

"Margaret's in custody, and Parker's body is on the way to the morgue." Reyes let him know. "Joey's not back yet?"

"Not yet. Soon." He hoped. Jack needed to hold his son.

Reyes glanced at Alana. "Is she okay?"

Jack nodded, though he didn't know if she truly was.

"And you?" Reyes questioned. "Are you hurt?"

"No."

Reyes looked concerned. "You were just doing your job, Jack."

No, he had been doing a lot more than his job. He'd been protecting Alana and ultimately Joey. That's how he'd get through this.

The medic bandaged Alana's knee and started to work on the large scrape on her elbow.

"I found a cell phone jammer in Parker's car," Reyes continued. "You said you hadn't been able to make a call, and that explains why." He paused. "I also found some papers."

Jack looked at the man when he didn't continue. "What kind of papers?"

"I'm not a lawyer, but these were pretty easy to figure out. Parker was going to have Alana sign away her part of the family business. The money would have gone into an offshore account. My guess is that he would have moved the money around for a while to make sure it wasn't traceable to him. But in the end, he would have had a big payoff."

"That's why Parker kept me alive," Alana said.

Jack hadn't even realized she was listening, but she'd heard every word.

Yes, the money would have been motive to keep her alive. First, he'd drained her trust fund and investments. Parker had been smart to do it slowly so it hadn't raised any red flags. However, cashing in her business accounts would have alerted Sean, and that probably meant Parker intended to cash in the account as quickly as possible, hide the money and try to cover his tracks.

He nearly succeeded, too.

"Did my brother have anything to do with those papers?" she asked.

Reyes shook his head. "Doesn't look like it. Parker would have been the only one benefiting from this. But I think Parker did a darn good job convincing your brother you were crazy. That's why Sean pushed the judge so hard to have you recommitted. In his own warped way, Sean thought he was helping you and thereby helping himself and your company."

Jack saw the relief slide through her otherwise weary expression. This didn't mean her relationship with her brother was fine and dandy, but at least Sean hadn't endangered her.

"They put out the fire at your house," Reyes continued. "There's some serious damage. Everybody's already chipping in to get the repairs started. All of you can stay at my place until they're done. I can bunk with a friend to give you more room."

"Thank you." Jack meant it. He wasn't surprised by the man's generosity. Willow Ridge was home, and Reyes wasn't just his deputy but also his friend.

Alana stood the moment the medic finished, and even though she winced as she got off the examining table, she quickly made her way to them. "What about Dr. Bartolo?"

"He called me on the way over. Said it was on the news about Parker being killed. He says now that he's not in danger, he's coming back." Reyes paused. "He might have to face charges for his role in the diamond deal."

Maybe. But Jack was betting that if the doctor had any info about Parker being dirty, Bartolo could trade that for immunity or probation. Not a bad outcome considering the alternative. Parker would almost certainly have tried to kill Bartolo so he could eliminate anyone who could connect him to the diamonds.

"So we're really safe," Alana said.

"We're safe." Since she didn't look too steady on her feet, Jack eased his arm around her waist.

"I knew we were. I mean, you wouldn't have sent for Joey if all weren't well. But it's nice to hear it aloud. To know that all the pieces are in place." She came up on her toes and kissed him.

Jack was pleased with the response, but he was sure that little display of affection surprised his deputy. Reyes fought back a smile. "I guess I should be going—"

"I'm in love with you, Jack," Alana said.

Now it was Jack's turn to be surprised. He stared at her.

She wasn't shaking. Her eyes were clear and focused. "When I was in that car with Parker and thought I was going to die, I regretted not telling you that I loved you. So I'm telling you now." She glanced at Reyes. "Sorry. I should have waited until Jack and I were alone, but I didn't want to waste another second."

Reyes continued to fight that smile. Jack didn't have a clue what to say or do. And Alana just stood there, waiting for a response.

From the other end of the hall, Jack heard familiar voices. He glanced over his shoulder and confirmed that Sheriff Tanner, Tessie and Joey had arrived. Alana stepped away to hurry to them, but Jack caught her arm.

He didn't want to waste any more time.

"I'm in love with you, too," he told her.

That stopped Alana. And it had Reyes moving quickly away.

Alana smiled. "You mean that?"

"With all my heart."

Her smile widened. "That's a lot." She hooked her arm around his neck and pulled him to her for a long, lingering kiss.

"Da-Da," Joey called out.

Jack wanted to hold his son, but he had to do something else first. Even if meant doing it in front of an audience.

"Will you marry me?" he asked Alana.

Despite Joey's chatter and the fact that Reyes, Sheriff Tanner and Tessie were only inches away, Alana didn't take her eyes off Jack. In her eyes, he could see her love for him.

He could also see their future.

"Yes, I'll marry you."

Jack hadn't realized he was holding his breath, waiting for that answer. This time, he was the one to initiate the kiss. He pulled her back into his arms and reminded her of just how much he loved her.

"Da-Da," Joey insisted. The little boy reached out, and both Alana and Jack took him, each of them cuddling an arm around Joey.

"I'll have to teach him how to say *Mama,*" Tessie volunteered.

"Ma-Ma," Joey blurted out, and then clapped as if very proud of himself.

Jack was certainly proud of him. His son had more than enough room in his heart for both a mom and a dad. He didn't feel threatened that he was losing Joey. He felt…complete.

Tears started to shimmer in Alana's eyes, but Jack knew they were tears of pure happiness.

Joey had been the one to bring them together, but it was the love that Alana and he felt for each other that made them more than just Joey's parents. That love had made them something Jack had always longed for.

A family.

* * * * *